Decoying Waterfowl

Other Books by A. C. Becker, Jr.

DECOYING WATERFOWL
WATERFOWL IN THE MARSHES
GULF COAST FISHING
LURE FISHING
BIG RED/CHANNEL BASS FISHING
GAME AND BIRD CALLING

Decoying Waterfowl

A. C. Becker, Jr.

South Brunswick and New York: A. S. Barnes and Company
London: Thomas Yoseloff Ltd

A. S. Barnes and Co., Inc.
Cranbury, New Jersey 08512

Thomas Yoseloff Ltd
108 New Bond Street
London W1Y OQX, England

Library of Congress Cataloging in Publication Data

Becker, Jr., A. C.
   Decoying waterfowl.

   Bibliography: p.
   1. Decoys (Hunting). 2. Waterfowl shooting.
I. Title.
SK335.B4 1973   799.2'44'028   74-37805
ISBN 0-498-01070-8

Printed in the United States of America

This one
is for two of the finest of waterfowlers,
Ray Bowen and Joe Lagow.

Contents

Preface

Decades ago when waterfowl were so plentiful that neither bag or possession limits were necessary, there were many, many places where gunners could get their birds without so much as setting out a single decoy. They simply stationed themselves in local flyways between feeding and resting grounds and banged away at the birds as they traded back and forth. This was true even at a time when other gunners in the same general areas were setting out huge rafts of decoys. Almost without exception the hunters with the huge rigs were market gunners, men who had to make every shell count in order to show as much profit as possible for their work. These market shooters were not above allowing a big flock of ducks or geese to land on the water. Then when all the "heads were in a line" so to speak, they cut loose and raked the birds on the water. It was not uncommon for them to kill or cripple a half dozen birds with a single shot.

Equally and almost without exception those gunners who took a flyway stand and shot birds as they traded back and forth were the sportsmen of the era. It was considered then as now very unsportsmanlike to shoot waterfowl on the water, unless it was to finish off a cripple. The only sportsmen who bothered with decoys in those bygone days were the extremely wealthy. Usually their hunting entourage included a sharecropper or trapper and his kids. The adult toted the heavy sacks of decoys, while the poor fellow's kids retrieved the downed birds. Although the rich hunter may have been highly sportsmanlike about killing the ducks and geese, his attitude toward those helping hands, who were usually known by first name only, was almost that of master to slave.

There still exist in this world places where the hunter regards the working help as serfs, and there are still a few areas where a hunter can take a stand, without decoys, and bag all the ducks he wants simply by popping them as they trade back and forth. These places of plenty are usually fabulous to such a degree that only the extremely

9

rich can afford such hunts. This book is not written for these people. Instead it is written for the working man, whose waterfowl hunting arsenal may include a single shotgun, an assortment of oddlot decoys and a hundred dollars budgeted for shells, license and fees for a season's hunting.

Waterfowl decoys are like fishing lures. Each can be highly realistic, but neither will be deadly if presentation is out of character. If results are to be obtained, the decoy or fishing lure must be presented in such a manner as to cause a reaction from the game. Expertly shaped and authentically painted decoys cease to be thoroughbreds and become little more than range ponies when they are used haphazardly.

A waterfowler who always brings in game is often said to be a lucky hunter. Why is he lucky? The answer is he knows what he is doing. He calls on personal experiences and knowledge of the sport. He makes his own luck.

There is no great mystery about using decoys properly. All one need do is watch ducks in the field, remember what he saw and then transpose this knowledge into his decoy rig. He will quickly discover there is far more to the use of decoys than just spotting them in a V or fish hook formation facing into the wind.

I live on the upper Texas coast. Each fall and winter skeins of ducks and geese stain the skies over the marshes and coastal bays. The good fortune of being a newspaper outdoor writer enables me to spend almost as much time in the field as some professional guides, and at least half of that time is spent just watching and observing.

The point that stands out most vividly is that ducks, like people, are creatures of habit. True, there are always nonconformists in any group, but for the most part the majority of ducks and geese of a given species are fairly predictable as to what they will do under a given set of circumstances.

You can see ducks and geese at the zoo or in an aviary garden. Regardless how realistic the architects lay out these areas, the inmates are still captives. They act the part of captives—feeding, loafing, and sleeping on schedule. All a person really gets to see are the colors of the birds.

My observations throughout this book are based on some 30 years of waterfowl hunting. I've watched ducks and geese before and after the hunting seasons, and I've seen plenty over the barrel of a shotgun. The characteristics of birds in the field are as different from those in the aviary garden as night is from day. The characteristics of birds during the off-season as compared with those during the hunting season come in many shades of gray. The hunter who desires to be called the "lucky" fellow by his associates must know these mannerisms and how to incorporate them into his hunting.

This book undertakes the task of road-mapping the way to better waterfowl hunting through the use of decoys.

Special credit and recognition is due Bertha Gill, who makes up display advertisements at the *Galveston* (Texas) *Daily News*. Miss Gill penned out the numerous sketches illustrating decoy placement and the attitudes of various waterfowl.

Many of the photographs in this book are the result of field trips made under the guidance of Joe Lagow of Anahuac, Texas. Joe manages the Barrow Hunting Preserve, the oldest waterfowl hunting ranch in Texas. Joe spent countless hours guiding me over thousands of acres of marshes and waterfowl habitat. He has spent a lifetime associated with waterfowl as a hunter, a guide, manager of a waterfowl hunting preserve, and breeder of waterfowl. A good amount of the information in this book stems from long discussions I've had with Joe Lagow.

A. C. BECKER, JR.

Galveston, Texas
July, 1971

Decoying
Waterfowl

1

A Sight to Behold

A dozen indistinct shapes undulate gently on the wide expanse of water riffled only by the light wind filtering through the tall stands of cane and rushes that guard the shoreline. The sky ahead is still black; the sky behind is toned in gray. A muskrat, its hunger satiated at a nocturnal feast, vees across the pond toward its den for rest and sleep. The swells caused by the swimming marsh creature widen, and the dozen shapes, now assuming duck-like proportions, begin to bob lifelike as the wake spreads like a wave over the pond. In the distance the coot chorus decreases as the darkness wanes, and more night creatures settle down to pass the day in seclusion.

And then suddenly overhead there is a whistling and whirring of wings—so close you can almost feel the wind created by the rapid beat. The sound comes unannounced and vanishes as quickly as it came. Because of the diminishing darkness you cannot yet see the source of the sound. But you know what it is anyhow: teal, and a big bunch. That fast wingbeat gave them away. Will they return? Did they see the dozen shapes on the water? You want them to return, but not too soon. It's still ten minutes before legal shooting time.

They return—from straight ahead. You see them skimming over the tops of the cane. Their wings are cupped and their feet are down. They dimple the pond as they splash down on the water. All heads are erect. Do they suspect something? No, it's a normal reaction. Several tip-up as they dabble the pond bottom for food. It's still too early to shoot, so you must watch. You lean forward for a better look, and in doing so clink the gun barrel against the thermos. The sound, foreign to the marsh surroundings, snaps all heads erect. That old drake nearest you is suspicious and takes to the air. The others follow suit. It's still too early to shoot, but you don't worry because you know they will return. They haven't been shocked by powder and shot—that will come later in the day.

Elsewhere in the marsh you hear the cough of a gun—once, twice, three times. You look at your watch and wonder if that guy's watch is three minutes fast or yours is three minutes slow. No matter, the day is just beginning. There is enough light now to make out the colors on the twelve duck-like shapes on the pond. They are your decoys. They look good, and you think that if you were a duck, you would certainly pay them a visit.

Another whistling of wings. This time from behind. The sound passes overhead and fades into the distance. Out of the corner of your eye you catch sight of the ducks. Another bunch of teal. Not so low as the first bunch that buzzed earlier but just about as many. Is it the same bunch? You suspect it is, and you bring your call to your mouth to sound the "come back" call. But there's no need to call. They have seen the decoys and wheel in a tight circle.

They're coming in; they're going to work the decoys. You tighten your grip on the gun, and in your mind you start the countdown. Yes, they're going to decoy for you note the bend of their necks. That lead hen is already dropping her feet. The others are taking the hint. Now wings are cupped. Tail feathers spread wide to reduce flying speed. Now is the time—they're right over the decoys.

You pick the drake to the left of the lead hen. Bam! It folds and plummets to the pond. The rest snap their legs and feet against their bodies and chandelle for altitude. They're making knots now, and you swing on another drake. Bam! They are flying faster than you supposed. Not the drake but a hen a few feet behind took the charge of shot and crumpled to the water. You swing quickly for a third shot, but as you squeeze the trigger you realize the range is too long. And you hope that third shot is a clean miss.

You debate picking up the game immediately, The marsh is alive with ducks. The crash of your gun signaled "flight time" to them. Singles, doubles, small bunches, big bunches of teal, mallards, black ducks and pintails cross and crisscross the sky. Some are in range for pass shots. You could fill out your limit in a matter of minutes, but you let them go unchallenged. You have been bred to hunting them over decoys, and pass shots would only be false notes in the concerto. You know the ducks are there, and you have the time to play the drama to its end. So you retrieve your game and once again settle in the blind.

The mallards and pintails are plentiful, and you set your mind to getting them only. It might be ten minutes, it might be a half hour before you get the target you desire, but the wait is worth it. In the interlude you watch the other ducks come and go.

Gunning ducks over decoys is the ultimate in waterfowl hunting. Above the author has retrieved a downed duck and watches another flight pass over far end of pond.

A half dozen green-winged teal buzz across the decoys like fighter planes strafing an airdrome. They turn for a second buzz, but sight something more interesting and vector away. A pair of shovellers, a drake and a hen, drop into the decoys as casually as the wife visits the supermarket. They waste no time and immediately start dabbling for food. That full-plumaged drake is one of the most colorful of all duck species, but oh how that big spatula-like bill spoils its profile. They are totally unaware of your presence. They swim to within 30 feet of your hide. Their minds are bent on one thing—choice tidbits off the bottom.

The sun is well up now, and the ripples on the pond twinkle like beckoning stars. A shadow passes swiftly across the surface. You hunker down and cautiously peer upward to scan the sky. There's the source. A drake mallard winging off to the left. He has seen the decoys and he is talking—"creep, creep, creep." It's a subdued call, and unless you knew what to listen for, you would miss it. You want to bring up your own call and in duck language tell that plump fellow that all is well for a visit.

But you can't. Your call will frighten those feeding shovellers, and when they flare into the air, they will only alarm that drake mallard. Under your breath you damn the shovellers that are now just 20 feet away. All you can do is wait and hope for the best. Your face is pressed against the cover of the blind, and you follow the movements of the mallard with your eyes. He's turning. He's crossing the stand of cane downwind and moving to your right. He's turning again and is going to circle behind you. Sixty yards. That's a long shot. You decide to wait. He vanishes behind you, and you fight the temptation to turn. But experience has taught you not to, and so out of the corner of your eye you watch to your left.

Was that dark shape a mosquito or a duck? It's clear now, the mallard, circling from the left. Now he's straight out ahead, downwind and turning in toward the decoys. Oh, those damned shovellers. They're paddling rapidly out to the middle of the pond. Will they flare and shy off the mallard? No, all is safe—they're just chasing surface aquatic life and are feeding again.

That greenhead is working in—his neck is bowed, his feet are down, his wings are cupped. Again the countdown. Seventy yards . . . sixty yards . . . fifty . . . forty . . . and now. Bam! The bird cartwheels to the water and hits with a mighty splash. The shovellers explode straight into the air as if bound for the moon. The hen bellows her loud alarm "quaack, quaack, quaack" and the pair become specks on the horizon.

And so now you have in the blind a pair of teal and a fat drake mallard. One more duck to fill out the limit and it's only eight o'clock. You'll be home in time for a nap before lunch.

Soon five more mallards wing over from straight ahead. They're too high to shoot, but the two hens in the flight are talking up a storm to the decoys on the pond. You answer in kind with your call, and quickly there is a regular coffee klatch going. They swing and circle the pond, high and out of range. They make a second circle, and this time lower and in range. But they're going to work the decoys, so you hold fire. Now they swing a hundred yards downwind and wheel back toward the decoys. You decide to wait them in close to pick the biggest drake in the flock. Suddenly sixty yards out they flare and tower for altitude as only mallards can. And in a few winks they are out of sight. Did they see your face? Or did you make an unintentional move or foreign sound? You'll never really know. They just took alarm and high-tailed away. Again experience tells you to write it off as part of the score, a suspense chapter in the book.

You debate whether or not to take a long pass shot at the next birds you see. But experience of hunting over the blocks makes pass shooting go against the grain. Again you elect to wait and let the mountain come to you.

The wait isn't so long as it seems. Soon there are gun barks elsewhere in the marsh, and you know that someone has put the birds to wing again. You scan the skies and pick up three dots in the distance. Are they coming or going? The dots grow larger. Now you can see the wing beat. They're big ducks, but are they mallards, pintails or black ducks? They're getting closer. Now they make a half-hearted circle over another pond, and their silhouettes—long necks and spike tails—identify them as pintails. They sheer off to the right and circle another pond. The characteristics are right. These ducks want to decoy. But something was wrong on the second pond because they zoom skyward. Now they angle in your direction. From their new altitude they must have seen your decoys and have decided to investigate.

Yes, they're coming, but gosh they're a hundred yards high. Well downwind they start to angle to your right. You know these ducks have been shot at recently and are wary. Still they are bent on coming down someplace. They circle high and well behind you and then reappear on your left. They cross downwind and again begin a circle from your right. And then they repeat it all in a third circle. The circles are tighter but the birds are still too high. The decoys must look good, but these birds are jittery, and they are now scrutinizing what lies around the pond. You hope the white handkerchief in your hip pocket is tucked down deep out of sight, but you dare not move a hand to check it. You hope you remembered to cover the bright aluminum thermos. But you dare not turn your head to look. A thousand thoughts race through your mind. Now far downwind the birds turn straight in for the decoys—but they're still a hundred yards high.

Oops, they're beginning to whiffle and are rapidly losing altitude. Again the countdown to trigger squeeze. One bird needed to fill the limit and you decide it will be a big one. The white front of that drake to the right stands out like a tuxedo shirt. No, the one to his left is a bigger bird. Bam! Dammit, jerked the gun and missed. A second bam! This time a puff of feathers and a pintail crashes into the decoys. Darn the luck. The tenseness of the long wait, your fumbled first shot made you swing your second shot on a hen instead of a drake. The remaining birds tower and fan to the horizon.

You have your limit, and as you pick up your decoys and gear, you add in your mind the hours it will be until the next day's hunt.

You have enjoyed a symphony that compares with the finest of musical scores, a drama that rivals the best on Broadway. But you enjoyed it as a participant, not a spectator. It was your production. The ducks were the actors, your decoys the stage settings, and you the director.

This is the kingly sport of decoying waterfowl. Once engaged to it, you marry it—and you never divorce it.

2
The Legacy

The market hunter, who passed into waterfowl archives in 1918, must shoulder part of the blame for the decline in duck populations. The degree of that blame lessens with the passage of time for now civilization, transformation of waterfowl habitat into industrial and urban developments, and pollution are taking their tolls. Nevertheless the old market hunter is still cussed by sportsmen. Yet if they took the time to delve into the history of waterfowling, they would learn the old codger left quite a legacy.

In brief, the old market shooter is the father of decoy duck shooting as we know it today.

Earliest American decoys were those used by the Indians. The Indians fashioned floats out of tules. Then leaving the heads and feathers on, they skinned ducks and stretched the skins over the forms. When the skins dried, they shrunk tightly on the forms. These were the decoys they used to lure birds within weapon range or into traps.

Decoys for ducks were also used in Europe, but here the main purpose was to entice the birds into traps. Birds were taken in great numbers for the trappers were actually market hunters. Decoys for the purpose of shooting ducks on a sporting basis also originated in Europe, but this was a hunting aspect reserved for the landed gentry. Only royalty had the necessary gun powder to burn for sport. Royalty used some artificial decoys but leaned far heavier on the use of tame and trained ducks.

These birds were tethered to stakes or wires and attracted wild ducks by their callings. They were referred to as "stool ducks." As hunting progressed, the term "stool duck" was shortened to plain

"stool," and in time this word was also applied to any kind of decoy—
live or artificial. The word today is a perfectly good one in the
waterfowl hunter's vocabulary. It is used most often when old timers
gather.

Use of live ducks as decoys came to America, and until the practice was outlawed, just about every sportsman waterfowler around
had a pair or two of "caller" ducks. These birds were usually mallards
and were often referred to as "English callers." You should listen
to old hunters speak lovingly of the "English callers" they once owned.

The American market hunter shot his ducks; he didn't bother
with traps. Some of the earliest ones used live decoys but only until
they discovered a more efficient way to lure birds into gun range.
The market hunter discovered that to get birds to work to him consistently he needed a lot of decoys on the water. Care and feeding
of live decoys took time and money. So he turned to the artificial
decoy. Early ones were hand made, carved out of wood native to
the area in which the man hunted. The market hunter learned that
the more decoys he set out, the more birds he attracted. Consequently
decoy rigs numbering into the hundreds were used. These earliest

*The old and the new in decoys. The two present-day molded plastic decoys at
right are more realistically shaped and painted than the older wooden models
at left.*

Note the differences in the heads of old and new decoys. Head of the molded plastic model at left is far more lifelike than the 50-year old wooden model at right. Glass eye in the wooden decoy is more realistic than the molded eye in the plastic model.

decoys were little more than crudely chopped blocks, and they were referred to as "duck blocks." The term has been shortened and remains in waterfowl vocabulary today as "block." It is proper to use it in connection with decoys.

The market hunter soon turned gunning over decoys into a science. He learned to carve his blocks and paint them to resemble the birds he sought. He learned the habits and characteristics of ducks, and then incorporated this into decoy placement and formations. His was a business where every miss cost him money.

The market hunter is now just a fragment in history. He slaughtered ducks, and he is responsible for the setting of seasons and bag limits. There's no denying that. He did good, too. He taught us how to use decoys. And because of this he certainly doesn't deserve a totally dark page in waterfowl history.

Antique decoys used by the market hunters don't compare with the expertly detailed and plumaged models that roll off assembly lines today. Still the old market shooter's rig had an allure few modern day hunters copy. It is so basic and obvious that it is frequently overlooked.

Can you guess what it is? It will become obvious if you go afield —without a gun—and just observe waterfowl.

The fact stands out that birds in a flock rarely assume identical poses simultaneously. For any given species the birds will have their heads, necks and bodies arched in various attitudes. Only when they are curious or frightened will every bird in the flock strike a regimented pose.

Going back to the market hunter we find he had decoys from many sources—home made, factory, stolen. They were in all stages of repair. Individually some were very shoddy looking, but when the conglomeration was spread, the rig became extremely lifelike and enticing to flying birds.

Individually today's factory decoy is a beauty in figure and artistry. But when several dozens of these same beauties are grouped together, the overall appearance can be as stereotyped as the Palace Guard.

This is no condemnation of modern decoys. Far from it. They are terrific, and they get desired results. Any condemnations in order must be leveled at the hunters themselves.

Far too many modern hunters misuse decoys. There's more to it than just pitching a bunch out on the water. This will bring in a few birds, and if the hunter has never shot over a proper decoy set, he probably will be satisfied with the results. But again after spending a small fortune on guns, shells, calls, hunting clothes, and decoys, why be satisfied to go in the second class coach? Moving up to first class is simply a matter of knowing waterfowl characteristics.

Decoys are inanimate objects. They can be placed out to look like statues or the real things. This is where the waterfowler fits into the picture. If he is to enjoy maximum pleasure over his decoys, he must know what kinds to use, how many to use, and where and how to place them. This is the meat of this book.

Succeeding chapters take up the call of the "where, when, why and how" to use decoys to attract waterfowl.

But before moving on a personal experience is necessary to illustrate a point.

"Dad, those ducks didn't circle round and around before they landed. You said they would in your book."

The scene was on the Anahuac (Texas) National Wildlife Refuge. The time was approximately six weeks after the close of the hunting season, and the reason for the visit was picture taking.

Obviously my youngest daughter Laura, who would rather hunt and fish with dad than be a girl, had been reading some of the rough drafts for this book. Now she sought an explanation for the incongruity.

The reader of this book is very likely to get the same impression if he goes waterfowl watching either before the hunting season or well after it closes. There is a decided difference in duck characteristics between unmolested birds and those who have been chased repeatedly by charges of shot.

Therefore throughout the various chapters, unless otherwise stated, the characteristics and mannerisms of birds discussed will pertain to birds made leery by repeated gun fire.

3

That Anatidae Family

Ducks are ducks. They all belong to one big happy family—the *Anatidae*. Certain broad similarities are shared by all of the species within this family. These earmarks include (1) four toes on each foot, three webbed with the fourth small and free, (2) flat bills, (3) short legs set wide apart, (4) dense feathers over a heavy layer of down, and (5) the ability to live in a watery environment.

Although they are all in the same family, one can't refer to the various species as being brothers and sisters. There is remarkably little hybridization of the clans. It would be better to refer to the different species as cousins, for while certain general characteristics may be similar, there are others of marked difference. For example, duck sizes scale from the tiny green-winged teal to the heavyweight mallard, canvasback and common eider. Then there is the full palette of colors on the vividly multihued drake wood duck down to the drab, dark scoter.

There are 38 species—or cousins—of the *Anatidae* family on the North American continent. These fall into two major groups—the puddlers, also called dabblers, and the divers—plus two minor groups. Each of the 38 tribes has its own distinct habits and characteristics. These lineaments can overlap to some degree, but each species combination is quite individualistic. If the waterfowl hunter is to lure ducks within gun range over his spread of decoys, he must first know the general traits and idiosyncrasies of the two major groups— puddlers and divers. This will put him in business.

(The two minor groups are sea ducks and fish-eaters. These birds have such a limited range and are of such poor table quality that they are seldom hunted. Of the two minor groups, the sea ducks are hunted

With some species of ducks the tendency on the water is for the hens to take the lead. Note the blue-winged teal hens are the leaders in the above photo. The drakes have the distinctive white half-moons on their faces.

These blue-winged teal are suspicious and they bunch up as they swim toward the middle of pond. Often a single duck will hide itself near vegetation at water's edge as in the case of the drake blue-winged teal in lower center of photo.

the most, but here again this gunning is confined mainly to the northern Atlantic and Pacific seaboards. The fellow gunning in Kansas might see an errant sea duck once in a lifetime.)

In later chapters in this book the flight and decoying mannerisms of major species within each major group will be discussed in detail. But before moving to these, it is necessary to bring out the general traits of these groups.

Puddler ducks are surface-feeders, and as the name suggests, these ducks favor small, shallow inland lakes, ponds and marshes. They are unlikely to go to wide open water expanses out of sight of land or to sea water. When they do, it is only to rest briefly; not to feed. Because of their inclination to restricted water areas often surrounded by tall vegetation, they are specially endowed for fast getaways. They take flight by leaping vertically in a single bound. Their descent to the water or land can be almost as vertical. They can be said to have helicopter qualities.

Since their legs are set a little forward of center, they have good body balance and are able to walk well on land. This gives them locomotion to forage as efficiently on land as in water. This adaptability to land movement is utilized to the fullest when there are grainfields, farm crops and lush grasses in an area. Although there are several exceptions, puddle ducks as a group feed more on vegetation than on animal matter. This in itself is the reason many waterfowlers prefer puddlers to divers for table fare.

Diving ducks are especially adapted for feeding on underwater matter and favor water areas far more open and less surrounded by tall vegetation than the puddlers. Divers will readily feed and rest in salt water and can often be found rafted a considerable distance out to sea. Birds in this group differ from the puddlers in that they have larger feet and shorter legs, which are located to the rear of the bird's body. Consequently they have poor balance and are so awkward on land that they seldom visit crops or cultivated fields. The waterfowler can attract puddlers to his decoys even when the rig is spread in a dry grainfield. Puddler decoys strategically spotted in a dry grainfield can turn it into duck garden of the Hesperides. The divers will work this same field only if it is sheeted over with water. The fact that divers spend most of their lives on the water means birds in this group will feed heavily on animal matter. The exceptions are the canvasbacks and redhead, species that dine mostly on vegetation.

Diving ducks have shorter wing spans than the puddlers and a faster wing beat. They also fly locally at less altitude than the puddlers, but in migration flights they form definite formations and fly at considerable altitudes. Divers lack the 'copter traits of the puddlers. They are unable to drop straight down, and also lack the ability to

*The two shovellers are "fluffed up" in a restful pose. The indistinct birds in
the distant background are coot.*

bound up vertically. They are like the conventional airplane in taking
off in that they need to build up air speed. Their takeoff is one of a
rapid wing beat coupled with fast paddling of the feet as they run
across the water. This, of course, means they need room ahead for
takeoff. They may be awkward getting into the air, but once up they
are strong, fast flyers.

Sea ducks—a minor group—are those adapted to salt water and
the open sea. They fly low in masses locally but high during migration.
Their migration paths follow the coastlines. Most have difficulty
getting off the water and do so after a rather long and awkward taxi.
Airborne they are strong, fast flyers. Except for the eiders, sea ducks
are dark, drab colored birds. They dine mainly on marine life, hence
the flesh has a strong smell and taste.

There is still another minor group of ducks specialized for underwater pursuit of marine life. These fisheaters are the mergansers,
birds with streamlined bodies and serragated bills. These birds are
so fish-tasting that they are not worth taking, and few waterfowlers
bother to hunt them.

A little knowledge of duck migration can be invaluable to the
waterfowler when it comes to spotting the decoys around his blind.
It will give him the clue as to whether the rig should be predominantly

drakes, hens or a mixture of the sexes.

The trait possessed by waterfowl of following the same migration paths and using the same nesting and wintering grounds year after year has long been thought to be an inherited faculty. Some present day naturalists, however, don't subscribe to this theory completely. They contend the older birds teach the youngsters the route. This is perhaps true in the case of geese, where family ties are strong and birds travel in family groups. But this may not apply to all ducks, for in some species the adults and young birds migrate at different times. The young and immature birds of some species are the first to start southward migrations to wintering grounds. This is why some clans are so easy to lure to decoys. There are marked exceptions in this migration pattern in the case of pintails and blue-winged teal. The adult drakes of these species head south first. Consequently a decoy spread early in the season should have a correspondingly large number of drakes. Mallards and black ducks often begin to pair off during the tail end of the hunting season in the southern tier of states. This dictates that near the end of the season a decoy spread should have a near-equal show of hens and drakes.

A 400mm telephoto lens was necessary to catch these two mallards unaware and at play. The hen at left is busy washing her feathers.

When ducks are suspicious they hold their heads high. Note the alarmed attitude of the drake pintail. Hen pintail is in the foreground swimming away from the camera.

These coot and two shoveller ducks (right) are suspicious. Note how all heads are erect and how all the fowls are swimming toward center of the pond.

A general habit of both puddlers and divers of all species is to leave resting spots early in the morning to head for feeding areas and then return to the resting spots again late in the afternoon. Thus the waterfowler will find it easier to pull ducks to decoys early and later in the day than at high noon.

This knowledge of general habits can make for a more proficient hunter, who in turn can become the expert waterfowler if he furthers his education to include a study of the mannerisms of the various species within the general groups.

It would be impractical to go into character references on each of the 38 species of ducks on the North American continent. To begin with many species are quite restricted in their range and are available to very few hunters. For example, waterfowlers along the Gulf Coast and in the interior states very rarely ever see any of the scoters. These birds are found only on the upper portions of the Atlantic and Pacific Coasts. Or consider the common eider, which winters only along the upper New England coast. Even more restrictive is Steller's eider, a sea duck that rarely comes south of the Aleutians.

Therefore throughout this book character references will be confined to species that have considerable to universal range in North America.

Eighteen species are grouped in the puddler class, and these include the following: mallard, black duck, pintail, green-winged teal, blue-winged teal, cinnamon teal, gadwall, American widgeon, European widgeon, mottled duck, wood duck, shoveller, ruddy duck, masked duck, Mexican duck, mallard hybrid, fulvous tree duck, and black-bellied tree duck.

Species in the diver group include canvasback, redhead, lesser scaup, greater scaup, ring-necked duck, common goldeneye, Barrow's goldeneye, bufflehead, old squaw, and harlequin duck.

Sea ducks number seven and include white-winged scoter, common scoter, surf scoter, common eider, Steller's eider, king eider and spectacled eider.

The fish-eaters are the common merganser, red-breasted merganser and hooded merganser.

Landing and takeoff characteristics of puddle and diver ducks are illustrated in the sketches on the following page.

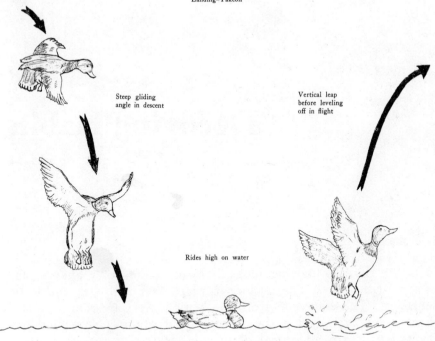

PUDDLE DUCK

Landing–Takeoff

Steep gliding
angle in descent

Vertical leap
before leveling
off in flight

Rides high on water

DIVING DUCK

Landing–Takeoff

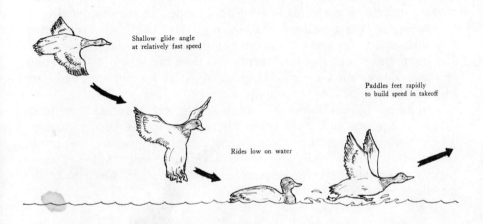

Shallow glide angle
at relatively fast speed

Paddles feet rapidly
to build speed in takeoff

Rides low on water

4

Decoying Habits

Only one thing holds true about decoying ducks—they always come in against the wind. The manner in which they approach and finally set differs. The difference is major when puddlers are compared with divers; but even within the broad classifications of puddlers and divers, there are additional decoying characteristics of the various species.

In general puddlers tend to fly high and circle or figure eight over a decoy rig before making their final approach, while divers tend to buzz low across a decoy rig and then swing into a very wide circle prior to the actual decoying. These are important points to keep in mind if you are to get birds in range. For example, have the patience to remain hidden and stone-still when puddlers wheel overhead. Resist the temptation to blast away at long range. Instead wait until the birds near the end of their approach, jam on air brakes and drop their feet. At this point they will be ten to fifteen feet off the water, moving quite slow and thus offering cinch shots. In the case of divers, skip trying to bag a bird on that buzzing pass. The birds are moving too fast, and they won't be in range for more than a few seconds. Let them make the pass, circle wide and then take them as they come in much slower on their final approach. At this point the birds are likely to be only a few feet off the water.

Although puddle ducks will work to big water areas, they do so around the points and in the coves where the water is usually shallow. The exception is the pintail, which often raft in large concentrations in the middle of bays, lakes and reservoirs. These open water raftings usually occur when the birds have been shot at a lot. They go to the middle bays to rest and not to feed.

This hunter is paddling out to set decoys in open space in flooded timber stand. This is an excellent place for puddle duck species like mallards, teal and wood ducks.

Puddlers have a decided preference for small water areas. Mallards, black ducks and teal seem to delight in dropping into potholes that may be no more than a few feet in diameter. They have no objections to dropping into these potholes even when the holes are surrounded by tall marsh vegetation. Mallards in particular will drop straight down through a tall timber stand to get to a cozy body of water. If the water is there, these ducks will often be found in rather dense thickets. Other puddler species like pintails, gadwalls and baldpates dislike flying low over timber stands. They like small water areas, but they prefer the area to be free of tall vegetation. These species have the common habit of nervously eyeballing the horizon in all directions.

Puddler ducks don't like deep water, and in their case any water over two or three feet in depth must be considered deep. These ducks feed by tipping up rather than diving. They do not like to dive completely under the water to feed, yet some are good divers and resort to diving when too crippled to fly and in seeking to escape an enemy.

The legs of these ducks are located toward the middle of their bodies; consequently they are able to walk fairly well. When undisturbed, they are likely to walk out on the bank and some distance on the adjoining land area to feed and rest.

Diving ducks, on the other hand, have a decided preference for open water areas where the water may be of considerable depth. The divers dislike having to fly over tall vegetation in making their approach to light on the water. Whereas the puddlers have the ability to drop almost straight down, the divers with their shorter wing span need to make an airplane descent to land. Puddlers have the ability to bound straight up into the air in taking off, and they can gain altitude swiftly in tight circles. Divers, however, have less helicopter in them, and they have to take off with a combination of running feet and flapping wings to build up air speed. Thus they need open water space ahead for takeoff room. The puddlers because of greater wing span have fairly good gliding ability. Divers have poor glide angles and must continuously maintain some sort of wing beat in order to prevent a crash landing.

Diving ducks' legs are located to the rear of their bodies; as a result their balance is poor. Consequently these ducks are poor walkers. They will walk onto a bank to feed or sleep, but they are very clumsy, and will stumble and fall all over themselves. When spooked on land, they are awkward and have difficulty in becoming airborne.

These same legs and feet, whether they belong to puddlers or divers, can telegraph to the hunter what a bird plans to do. Ducks not yet ready to set will fly with their legs flush back against their bodies with their feet tucked in under their tails. They signal their intentions to come down by extending their legs out beside their tails and spreading their webbed feet. This adds wind resistance and enables them to throttle flying speed.

Now to the flying and decoying characteristics of the most popular duck species.

MALLARD: This duck, except during migration flights, flies in gun-range altitude—a hundred to two hundred feet. It rarely flies in a straight line and does a lot of meandering. When approaching a decoy rig, it will meander out of range before circling over the spread. Once it makes up its mind to decoy, the mallard will make its final approach turn over the blocks at the tail end of the rig, and then rapidly lose altitude to set at the front of the spread or to the inside near the front. If the rig is split into two sections with an open slash of water immediately in front of the blind, the bird is likely to drop into this area. In the final drop the mallard comes down almost vertically the final ten to fifteen feet and lights on the water with scarcely a splash. Hens tend to decoy closer to shore than do the drakes.

BLACK DUCK: This duck has habits similar to those of the mallard, but it is far more wary in its approach to the decoy rig. It tends to go down near the front of a spread but well outside of it.

PINTAIL: This is an extremely graceful duck, and it is a symphony of motion when it decides to work to the decoys. Pintails fly high, well out of gun range for pass shooting. If the flight has a decided V formation, it is not likely to decoy. When pintails do decide to work

Some puddle duck species readily decoy to land areas. These pintails are working to the grass area ahead of the speckled-belly goose at lower left of photo. The pintails include two drakes and two hens.

Late in the hunting season in the south some duck species show signs of pairing off. These pintails are already paired. The photo was taken several days before the end of the Texas hunting season in early January.

a spread, they will wheel and figure eight over a rig at extreme gun range. Just be patient and wait. This is a wary duck that may circle and wheel over the blocks many times before dropping down into effective range. When this bird decides to come down, it will do so in a zig-zag side-slipping manner, and like the mallard will drop almost straight down the final ten to fifteen feet. In spite of all its grace, this bird hits the water with considerably more splash than the mallard.

TEAL: This duck, and especially the green-winged species, is the easiest of all puddlers to entice to decoys. Both green-winged and blue-winged teal fly low in tight bunches. The blue-wings in particular fly very low, and in crossing an area will dodge over and around brush, trees and so forth. The average hunter is not likely to see the approach of teal. First thing he knows there is a whistling of wings just a few feet overhead. The temptation to grab the gun and get off a shot in a hurry is the wrong move to make. Forget it. If the teal didn't see you or something in the area that spooked them, the bunch will fly well downwind, turn and head back into the decoys. And they come in with a lot of splashing, seemingly all trying to hit the water at the same time. A flight of mallards, black ducks or pintails rarely ever hits the water all together. They sort of dribble down. Green-winged teal are likely to drop right into the body of the decoy rig, whereas blue-wings will work more to the outside.

Puddle ducks like these mallards prefer to feed and dabble in shallow water. Attempting to decoy mallards to deep water is a lost cause.

GADWALL: This bird, also known as the gray duck, has decoying habits similar to the mallard. An exception is a marked tendency to set well outside the rig.

WIDGEON: This duck, which is also called the baldpate, flies at medium heights and usually in a straight line. When it works to decoys, it will nervously buzz the rig several times, and then go set down some place in the far distance. The best thing to do with these ducks is to take them on the second pass, for odds are poor that they will give you decent decoying shots. This duck will readily come down in grainfields and then graze across the land like cattle.

CANVASBACK: The only time these diving ducks fly high is when they are migrating; otherwise their flights are within a few feet of the water. When they approach a land area they increase altitude but rarely do their flying above gun range. If these ducks are flying in line or distinct V formation, they are not about to decoy unless the hunter is shooting over a rig composed of several hundred blocks. Canvasbacks set on decoying will approach swiftly from downwind and pass low and fast outside the rig. A hundred or so yards upwind these birds will turn back over the water and circle wide to make their final approach from downwind. The hunter will know they are about to decoy, for the flight will lose all semblance of formation. They usually decoy ahead of or to the outside of the spread. An important thing to remember about canvasbacks is that they don't like to make their final approach over land. This means there must be a lot of open water behind or downwind of the decoy spread.

BLUEBILLS: These ducks are more properly known as scaup—lesser and greater. They rarely fly in any sort of formation and like the canvasbacks they fly low over the water and just a little higher over land masses. Their decoying habit is one of buzzing the spread, often from upwind. If the wind is strong, they are likely to continue another hundred to two hundred yards downwind before turning tightly to head back into the wind and toward the decoy rig. They have a tendency to set at the head of the spread, but when the wind is quite strong, they are more likely to set outside the tail end of the spread and then swim into it.

REDHEAD: If there was ever a fool duck, the redhead has to be the one. It is a species that shows little caution in decoying and will frequently do so with the hunters standing right out in the open. Redheads may pass over a spread and then circle back to come in to set. More often, however, this bird comes in without either circling or crossing the spread. They have a habit of swooping down from considerable altitude with a rushing sound and plunking right down with the main spread of decoys. Hunters probably bag as many redheads jumping them out of the decoys as they do getting them coming in to the spread. This is the fool duck that you suddenly realize isn't a decoy when it starts swimming around, feeding and even pecking at the decoys. You never saw it come in; it just showed up. No need to grab frantically for the gun and knock over the coffee thermos in the process. Just take your time. You may even have to shout or throw something at the duck to make it flush off the water—that is, unless you find sport in shooting sitting ducks. Redheads, like bluebills, will readily work to a show of puddler decoys. Canvasbacks, however, will not truck with the puddlers. Cans are willing to fly over the puddlers, but they won't decoy with them. So if you want canvasbacks, your decoys must be of the diving duck species—canvasbacks, bluebills or redheads.

Whether the ducks are puddlers or divers, the hunter must pay close attention to the head and neck attitudes. As long as the neck is stretched out and the head extended like that of a race horse, the bird is not about to decoy. It is bent on making knots and going places. But when the neck is bent and the head held high, it is a different story. This is the bird getting ready to come down. Within seconds after the neck is arched, the bird will begin to lower its feet. Just a few feet from the water the bird will extend its legs forward and open its feet wide to spread the webs.

In their first pass over the decoy spread, divers are likely to have their heads and necks in the race horse attitude. Puddlers are more likely to start bending their necks on the initial circle over the spread, even though they may wheel several times before actually settling to the rig.

5

Rig Formations

You wouldn't go to the soda jerk behind the ice cream counter for help in making out your income tax return. His figures might please you, but more likely they would result in the IRS boys dropping by for a friendly audit.

Many hunters go on the assumption that a set of decoys will solve all their problems and put game on the table. They have the right idea, but they fail to cultivate the seed into germinating into something productive. The mere presence of decoys on the water may entice a few birds in range, but only if the birds are already abundant in the area hunted.

How and where the decoys are placed is what puts the fine cutting edge on the sword. Since this involves factors like wind, water conditions, duck species, duck habits, hunting competition and so forth, the situation can become almost as complex as the annual income tax return.

Waterfowlers know that ducks decoy into the wind and ride the water into the wind. It's important that they also know why. Facing into the wind allows ducks to make a fast getaway takeoff—a good idea if they wish to survive. The other reason is one of comfort. Ducks don't like to have their feathers turned or ruffled by the wind.

The hunter gets off the starting blocks right in placing his decoys facing into the wind. But then he can lose the race if the rig formation is all wrong. He can't afford to overlook duck habits, characteristics, likes and dislikes.

Ducks, whether they are puddlers or divers, like water, but they don't like rough water. When they have their druthers, they will always work and decoy to the calmest part of the pond, lake or bay.

Always keep in mind that your decoy is kept in place against wind, tide and current by means of an anchor. A duck isn't so endowed, and it can only keep in a particular area by means of constant paddling. This takes a good deal of energy, and a duck interested in either resting or feeding isn't going to cotton to constant paddling to do so.

How close a duck is willing to decoy to the shoreline depends upon the species. Puddle ducks—especially mallards, black ducks, and teal—show a willingness to come down in secluded, small water areas often surrounded by tall vegetation. Divers on the other hand will not decoy to this kind of water. They want open water and prefer to work to points that finger out from the shoreline.

A diver spread of decoys set near the shoreline in a small cove is incongruous with the habits of the species. Diving ducks that may work to this rig will do so far out of range. The hunter can change his luck to the good simply by moving that two hundred yards to the finger of land jutting out into the water and then setting his spread on the calm side. Then he'll get his diving ducks to work into easy gun range.

Best results with the puddler rig would be obtained by locating it in the cove—unless you're after pintails. This duck must suffer from claustrophobia for it shuns constricted coves. It will work far better to a spread of decoys off a point.

A duck's day can be divided into three not necessarily equal parts of flying, resting and feeding. Wild ducks go around dabbling and feeding almost as much as the chickens pecking around in the back yard. Therefore decoy placement must convey a special message to flying birds.

On a windless day, or when there are no water currents running, decoys set out in small groups are ideal. There is no formation to this spread. The decoys are clustered in groups of five or six, all groups being within gun range of the blind. If puddle ducks are involved, a small cluster on the bank is ideal. Purpose of this rig is to give flying ducks the impression that this is a peaceful place into which they can drop for a quick siesta. The same idea can be telegraphed to diving ducks by clustering the spread off a finger in the lake or bay. Spacing between decoys should be two to three feet, since resting and feeding ducks have a tendency to cluster closer together than ducks swimming toward some destination.

But to repeat, this cluster rig is effective only when there is an absence of wind and water currents. Ducks resting or feeding on calm water on such a day will face in all directions.

In a good wind or when currents are running all decoys will face in the same direction. Consequently the waterfowler should arrange his spread with definite formation. This formation can be a series of Vs or a loose fish hook, sometimes called the J set. The apex of the Vs and the bend of the fish hook point into the wind. The purpose of these patterns is to give flying ducks the impression that the decoys are swimming toward a feeding or resting spot. Both the V and fish hook patterns work well for diving ducks. The fish hook is the best set for the puddlers.

What kind of shooting do you enjoy most? Fast swing shots at birds zipping over the decoys? Or relatively slow moving shots at birds dropping their feet and braking wings just prior to settling on the water?

You can dictate style by decoy placement. For example, suppose you are shooting a cross wind, meaning the wind is blowing from your right to the left or vice versa. For fast swing shots at birds flying over the decoys, start the head of the spread well upwind. This can mean that birds actually settling to the water are likely to do so at rather long range upwind. Your hunting in this case will be a kind of pass shooting. If you want actual decoying shots, then start your spread immediately in front of the blind.

The direction in which the bend of the fish hook turns makes a big difference as to where the birds will decoy. When the hook is turned in toward the shoreline, puddle ducks generally work to the inside of the rig. Your targets will be close. There are exceptions with puddlers, especially in the case of pintails, gadwalls and widgeons. These species will almost always work to the open water on the seaward side of the shank. This means that if these are the predominant ducks in your area, your fish hook pattern should be one in which the bend turns away from the shoreline. Otherwise decoying birds may work so far seaward of the shank that they will be out of range.

The tail-end of a decoy spread—whether the formation is V or fish hook—should never be closer to the shoreline than the front of the rig. If it is, the impression from the air—which happens to be the duck's point of view—is that the decoys are swimming *away* from the shoreline. Birds will decoy to this set, but they will do so well away from the shoreline and possibly out of gun range. The proper set should have the head of the rig nearest the shore with the tail-end swinging outward. Ducks have a habit of wanting to decoy *ahead* of birds already on the water. The sole purpose of decoys is to get the birds in range. Why use a set that steers the birds out of range?

A decoy or two with an extra long anchor line is ideal for the tail-end of the spread. This long line will permit the block to tack back and forth in rather long sweeps. This extra bit of swinging is most tantalizing in attracting birds. It's a lot like that wiggly rubber skirt on the rear of a fishing lure.

Effective killing range of the 12 gauge gun is 60 yards. This is a long shot. The ideal range and the one that offers the most rewards to the hunter is 30 to 50 yards. The hunter must know how far to place decoys from the blind in order to get birds within this ideal range.

Regardless the formation used, always remember it will be several times longer than it is wide. Ducks just don't swim across the water on broad fronts in lines abreast like a Seventh Cavalry charge.

Let's take a typical example for the spotting of three dozen decoys in the fish hook pattern. The width of the formation should be about five to six yards. The length from the point decoy to the tail-ended is likely to be around 20 yards. When placing this rig before a blind, the nearest part of the width should be about 20 yards. This then makes the far side about 25 yards out. This will keep skitterish ducks that have a distinct tendency to work outside the rig still within effective gun range.

Using this set and spotting it so that the head of the spread is immediately in front of the blind, and if a great many decoys are used, means the tail-end blocks are likely to be anchored at extreme effective gun range, possibly even out of range. Don't worry about it. Very few ducks ever stool to the very rear of any rig. Those that do are almost always gut-shot birds just looking for a place to set.

Some hunters have trouble estimating range. Decoy placement can solve this one, too. Again using the spread described above, add one thing more: step off 60 yards straight out from the blind and spot it with a decoy. If your rig contains many dozen blocks, then mark the spot with two or three decoys. I call these "range" decoys. Anything that flies low over the water between the main spread and the "range" blocks is within killing range. In keeping with habits of duck species, I always use drake pintails for "range" blocks. No matter how many pintails plunk down on the water there are always several drakes that separate themselves from the crowd and take station 20 or so yards out from the main body. I don't know whether these birds are outcasts or just being snobbish. If these were geese, then it would be a sucker bet the birds away from the flock were watch ganders, quick to give alarm if they spotted danger. This isn't the case with pintails. Most of the time when pintails are frightened and take flight, the "loners" outside the main flock are among the last to rise.

Often blinds are built right out in the middle of a lake or bay. This would seem to violate the rule that ducks work to the center of the water only when they are nervous. This would be true if there was no blind out there. But when a lake or bay does have a blind or tiny island, ducks will regularly work to the shelter side of it. This is the side that offers protection from rough water. Some water-fowlers who own many dozens of decoys and who hunt from these middle-of-the-water blinds make the common mistake of completely surrounding the blind with decoys. True, it makes the blind less conspicuous and even allows the hunter some freedom of motion that flying ducks will neglect to notice. Unfortunately it can also mean that ducks are likely to decoy behind you or on your "blind" side. There may be no physical pain involved for the hunter, but this situation is as penalizing as football's blind-side clip.

This mass of decoys all around the blind can produce some Keystone Kop chases when cripples are involved. A couple of personal incidents bear repeating.

One involved a drake pintail I wing-clipped at long range. The sprig tumbled to the water well outside the rig. By all rights it should have started swimming toward the middle of the reservoir. But not that pintail. He paddled toward the rig, and, of course, I kept waiting for him to get in better range for the coup de grace. Then when I decided to finish it off, the bird dived. It swam underwater and came up right amongst the decoys. An easy 30 yard shot, but a shot that would also blast the decoys. The water was about knee deep, so I decided to run the bird down. Every time I got within 20 or 30 feet it would dive. That fool bird led me two merry chases completely around the blind. I fouled my feet in anchor lines and fell down twice. Meanwhile my host back in the blind was having the laugh of his life. He actually got to the point of cheering for the duck. I retaliated with references to his ancestors, although I must confess I got to laughing, too. It was a funny scene.

Then the blasted duck vanished and did what crippled sprigs so often do. It grabbed something on the bottom and hung there. Wounded pintails will do this and actually drown themselves. It's not a bird that surrenders easy. I finally located and grabbed the bird when I noticed one of the decoys doing the dipsy doodle. The bird had grabbed hold of the anchor line. In addition to a broken wing, a pellet had also struck the bird in the neck, and the bird was bleeding freely. Had it not been obvious it was going to die, I would have taken it home and splinted the wing. It would have been legal for I held a federal waterfowl breeder's permit at the time.

The other Keystone chase was an expensive one to the man who hosted the hunt. And he did it all himself. This time it involved a fat bluebill. It, too, swam into the decoys. Three times my host leveled down for the finishing shot. Each time a split second before trigger pull, the duck dived and each time the charge of shot Pearl Harbored a plastic decoy in the background. To add insult to injury the duck died from loss of blood. No finishing shot was ever needed.

There is more to this story. When my host leaned down to pick up the bluebill, he split his waders. I never got around to asking, but I certainly hope that duck was ultra supreme viand. It cost enough: four 12 gauge shells (12 cents each), three plastic decoys ($2.95 each), and waders ($14.95). That totals $24.34, and for a two-pound bluebill that averages out to $12.17 a pound, including feathers and all.

Always keep decoys spotted in one of three places—in front of, to the left of, or to the right of the blind. Never all around it. It just isn't good military strategy—look what happened to Custer at the little Big Horn.

Sketches on the following pages illustrate some of the rig patterns discussed in this and other chapters of this book. For sake of simplicity the number of decoys in the sketches are few in number. In practice more blocks are needed. For example in the "Mixed Diver-Puddler" rig seven decoys are indicated in the V portion (divers) and 12 in the fish hook. On open water areas these numbers should be doubled.

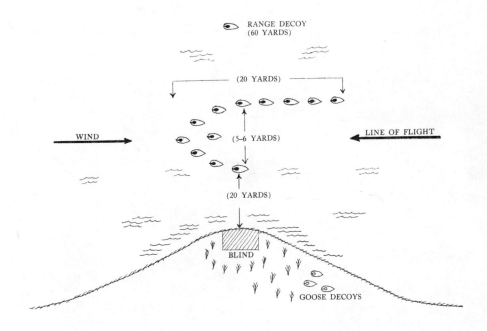

MIXED DIVER-PUDDLER
"V" and FISH HOOK RIG

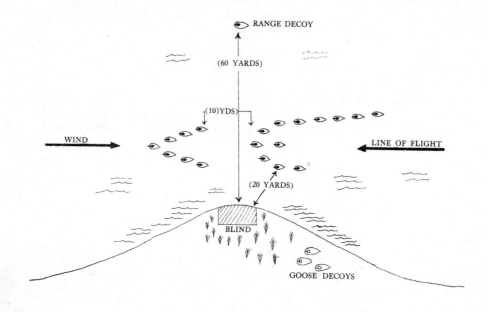

DIVING DUCK "V" RIG

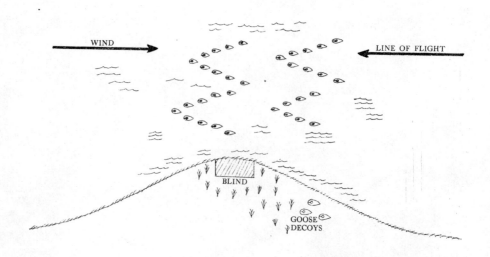

6

Shooting the Breeze

Wind direction, blind location and configuration of shoreline will determine the placement of the decoy spread. For one wind the rig may be directly in front of the blind. Another wind may necessitate stringing it off to one side or the other, or perhaps even dividing the rig.

Ideal winds are those blowing from either side or from behind the hunter. The waterfowler who faces directly into the wind would find his time better spent by staying at home.

Just look what this face-into-the-wind hunter has to battle. His decoys will face into the wind. This means the tail of the rig will be nearest the blind with the head extending out to long gun range. Furthermore he will be on the rough water side of the pond or lake, and it has already been pointed out in earlier chapters that ducks don't like to ride rough water. It may be redundant, but I feel this is something that can not be overemphasized. Normally ducks do not like to fly in strong winds. They do so only when chased into the air by hunters. A flying duck uses approximately eight times as much oxygen as it does when resting on the water. If the water is rough, the bird is going to use a lot of oxygen just paddling its feet.

All birds that work to the fellow shooting nose-into-the-wind will come in from behind him. Usually his first glimpse will be when the birds pass overhead. The normal reaction is to grab for the gun. The ducks see this movement in the blind, pour on the coal and are out of range before the poor fellow is ever able to mount the gun. His "chaser" shots will serve only to keep ammo company stock high.

If he doesn't spook the birds and they still decide to decoy, his shots will be at birds at long range. Furthermore they will be tail-end shots, and it is most difficult to kill a duck with a derriere shot.

A bird can be hard hit in the rump, and it won't die immediately. It can fly on for many hundred yards before giving up the ghost. This many hundred yards can mean a lost duck.

With what not to do out of the way first, let's switch over to spread placing when the winds are favorable.

On crossing winds go with V, fish hook or series of cluster formations. You can start the head of the spread immediately in front of the blind, although I prefer to start it 10 to 15 yards upwind. I also like to split the rig into two sections but not equal in number.

Let's consider an actual case. The wind is blowing across the blind from right to left, and I plan on setting out three dozen puddle duck decoys. I would place eight or nine blocks in a rough V, starting this spread some 10 to 15 yards upwind. When looking directly straight ahead from the blind, this small spread would be at an angle of about 45 degrees to my right. Then I would leave an open space of 20 to 30 feet immediately in front of the blind. Next I would start my remaining decoys in the second part of the spread, this time using the fish hook formation with the hook part turning inshore. The tail-end of the shank of the hook would loosely curve away from the shoreline. If the blind is located on a point, this shank can be extended straight back. In all probability the tail-end decoy in this second section would be at extreme gun range, possibly even out of range.

This split rig, I have found, is superior when ducks are skitterish. I always assume ducks are automatically skitterish and wary during the hunting season.

If the ducks have not been shot at recently and are not jittery, they are likely to decoy at the head of or to the inside of the small V spread to my right. The decoying characteristics of wary, often-shot-at birds is different. On a single spread they are likely to work outside the rig at rather long range. Yet when the spread is divided into two parts, these same wary birds have an affinity for that open slash of water between the sets. Perhaps their reasoning is that of the culprit who feels safest when lost in the crowd. It could be for an entirely different reason, but since ducks don't speak our language, I can only go on a supposition arrived at after more than 30 years of waterfowling.

During the course of a day it is unlikely that the wind will remain constant from the same direction. There may be variations of 20 to 30 degrees either way. This, however, offers no real problem, nor does it necessitate rearranging the spread. But any time the wind direction switch is 90 degrees or more, you'd better get out there and change the set to compensate.

If there is a 180 degree wind switch on the divided set mentioned earlier in this chapter, then the hunter must make amends by completely flip-flopping his rig. Otherwise he is not going to get any decent shooting.

Now let's take another actual case. Same blind and location as earlier described, only this time the wind is blowing directly from behind the hunter. Every shot here is going to be on a bird coming straight in. Man, these are real "meat" shots. Dead center that old mallard when he drops his feet and cups wings to chop air speed, and the bird will never know what hit him. Clean kills every time because the force of the charge hits the birds in their "vitalist vitals." No rump shots here. No time lost in this kind of hunting chasing down and finishing off cripples on the water. It's the exact opposite of the shooting the nose-into-the-wind hunter has.

Okay, so how do I spread the rig for this back-of-the-head wind?

A common mistake is to spread the rig almost line abreast on the assumption that all decoys must be kept within effective gun range. This is a grave error.

If I elect to go with a single spread, I would use either the V or fish hook, starting the front of the rig about 30 yards out from the blind. The tail-end would range offshore and well out of gun range. Ducks will work to any of three areas on this spread—immediately in front, left front or right front. In all fairness to the hunter let me point out that birds decoying immediately in front of the rig are clean kill or clean miss targets. They are usually so close that unless the bird is dead-centered, the shot is likely to be a clean miss. Remember if the bird is only 20 yards out, the diameter of the shot circle is rather constricted. When birds work in like this, the best way to take them is to start shooting before they clear the front of the rig. Also keep in mind that a duck dead-centered at any range under 20 yards is going to be a pretty shot-riddled hunk of meat.

Personally I prefer to split my rig for hunting this kind of wind— a small V to the right, another to the left, and then the main spread out front. In this case the head of the main spread would be started about 30 yards out. The small Vs would be started about 15 yards out from the shoreline with the distance between these spreads being some 20 to 25 yards. This open pocket is particularly attractive to nervous ducks.

Much of our hunting today is in areas frequented by both puddler and diver ducks. Thus any hunter who guns a body of water used by both classes should use the mixed rig.

Ducks may be ducks, but the various species are snooty about fraternization. So don't try to make a federal case by mixing your puddler and diver decoys all together. It just won't work. Duck species, like people, have likes and dislikes. Diving ducks, the canvasback excepted, will decoy to puddler ducks but they will not mingle closely in the group. Puddle ducks, on the other hand, seldom decoy to divers and show a marked dislike even to flying low directly over divers on the water. These things must be kept in mind when setting out the mixed rig.

Proper grouping calls for placing the diver decoys—canvasbacks, redheads and bluebills—in a series of Vs upwind and at the head of the rig. Leave that open slash of water in front of the blind, and then place the puddler decoys in a loose fish hook trailing downwind. This is the proper setting for shooting winds blowing from either side.

If the wind is directly from behind you, place the puddlers off to one side and the divers to the other. The head of the puddler rig should be about 30 yards out. The start of the diver rig should be around 35 yards out. Landing habits of the ducks dictate this. Divers come in like airplanes and need more landing space, while puddlers are capable of dropping almost straight down à la whirlybird. Divers also like open water ahead for takeoff room.

Diving ducks won't hesitate about flying low directly over the puddler decoys when working to the diver blocks up front. You can get some fine shooting at these birds as they jet over the blocks. They'll be just a few feet off the water.

Puddler ducks are less sociable when it comes to trucking with the divers. On the properly set divided rig—divers up front, open slash of water, the puddlers behind—the puddle ducks will invariably stool to the open slash.

But if the diver rig is downward in the rig, the decoying habits of the puddlers change. They will swing wide of the divers and decoy outside of or far to the front of the puddle rig. Either way they are likely to be out of range.

There are exceptions to all rules—notably in the case of widgeons, green-winged teal and redheads.

Green-wings nervously settle to a strict diver rig, hang around a few seconds and then scat. This is almost certain to happen in early morning shooting and before the sun gets up. Perhaps the eyesight of teal isn't what it should be, and they have difficulty in recognizing species in the semi-darkness.

Widgeons, which are also known as baldpates, will readily decoy to divers, especially so if the divers are feeding. Old market hunters call the widgeon the "poacher duck" because of the bird's habit of dropping in to steal vegetation pulled from the bottom by the diving ducks. This is a sight to behold and it is worth passing up shooting just to watch bluebills and redheads dive, bring up succulent vegetation, and then have a sassy baldpate snatch it away.

The redhead is a case all by itself. It will drop in readily on a 100 percent puddler rig, especially if the decoys are stylish pintails. Not only that, the redhead will plunk right down in the middle of the group—not up front or off to one side. The redhead is so easy to decoy that it amazes me that the species has managed to survive.

In a given area where both puddlers and divers abound, do you know species' habits for the amount of wind blowing?

On a dead calm day, the puddlers are more likely to fly than the divers. Divers tend to raft up in the middle of large water areas, and then stay there until something stirs them up. Under howling norther and small craft wind conditions, the puddlers do a lot of moving early in the morning, seeking out calm, secluded ponds. Then they will set and stay put. The divers, particularly bluebills, will do a lot of moving under strong wind conditions. They, too, search out calmer water. Their flights will be low over the water and will follow the configuration of the shoreline. Under strong wind conditions bluebills decoy with reckless abandon.

The ideal wind for all species is a moderate one—10 to 15 knots. Winds below this and down to around five knots are ideal for the puddlers. Divers tend to fly more on winds in excess of 15 knots. A dead calm is terrible for waterfowl hunting. The birds stay put until something frightens them out. By the same token the birds are not likely to move around in gale force winds. So use decoy species to fit the wind velocity when hunting an area used by both puddlers and divers.

Just as there are non-conformists in a group, there are also exceptions to this rule. I have already noted that diving ducks dislike working to secluded ponds surrounded by fairly tall vegetation. I also noted that canvasbacks in particular don't truck to puddle ducks. Well, all these rules went out the window on a hunt many years ago.

My hunting partner and I set out a spread of a dozen mallard blocks on a marsh pond that probably wasn't more than 60 feet in diameter. It was completely surrounded by cane 10 to 12 feet tall. And that cane was thick. All we had to do was step back into it a few feet, and we were completely hidden from sight. The nearest open water, the kind that diving ducks like, was a bay about three miles away.

It was dead calm when we set out the decoys and it was on a day when the weatherman had predicted a norther. The blow was due to hit in the afternoon, but as it so often happens in Texas, the norther had little respect for the weatherman. It barreled in about nine o'clock in the morning. Rain came down in sheets and stung like shot. And how that wind screamed. We estimated the wind at 50 miles per hour, but later learned it hit 60 and gusted to 75. On top of that a small tornado wooshed through the marsh about a mile from where we were hunting, but we did not know it at the time. The rain drumming on our foul weather gear drowned out all noises.

Frankly, we didn't expect to bag a duck. We just hunkered down in the cane to protect ourselves as best we could from the elements.

And then in the midst of all this ducks started dribbling into the decoys. Canvasbacks, canvasbacks, canvasbacks. They didn't case the joint. They just came sailing into the decoys, and, of course, we had limits in nothing flat. The weather was too violent to pick up decoys and head out of the marsh. We figured our best bet would be to ride it out. We had our limits, so we just watched more ducks stool to the decoys. Except for a few teal, all were canvasbacks, and at one time we must have had 50 ducks huddled on the water.

Obviously what had happened was the open bay—normally a canvasback playground—had become violently rough. The cans left it for more protected areas, saw our decoys and just piled in with them. Visibility was severely limited, but I suspect that morning the cans flew all over that marsh and landed on any water free of breaking waves.

It was around eleven o'clock before the front passed. Although the wind continued to blow around 20 miles per hour, the rain stopped and the sun broke out. The canvasbacks immediately vacated our pond. It took us about an hour to gather up the decoys and return to the car. Meanwhile we saw mallards flying all over the place, but not a single canvasback. The day was just one of those where waterfowl broke their own rules.

Back in the mid-1950s, when ducks were fairly plentiful, I had another against-the-rules hunt on a dead calm, 80-degree day. There were three of us in the party. The water was so calm the decoys appeared to be sitting on a mirror. According to duck general characteristics, it was a day when the birds were not supposed to fly. Yet fly they did. In a half hour of shooting we got our limits of drakes only—mallards, pintails, baldpates and redheads. I don't know what got the ducks moving so much. There was no other shooting anywhere in the area. I guess ducks are like people; sometimes they break the rules.

The following pages contain sketches showing blind and decoy placements for the same body of water under four different wind directions. If the diving ducks are not plentiful in the area, or if the pond is too small to be attractive to divers, omit using any diver decoys. However, if the water area is a large one and puddle ducks are scarce, then go with just the diver decoys. In this case where fish hook patterns marked "puddlers" are indicated change the set to the V rig.

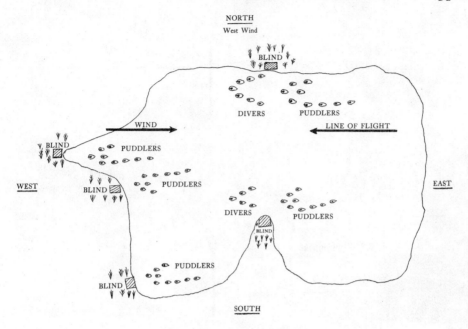

NORTH
West Wind

BLIND

DIVERS PUDDLERS

WIND LINE OF FLIGHT

BLIND PUDDLERS

WEST BLIND PUDDLERS EAST

DIVERS PUDDLERS

BLIND

PUDDLERS

BLIND

SOUTH

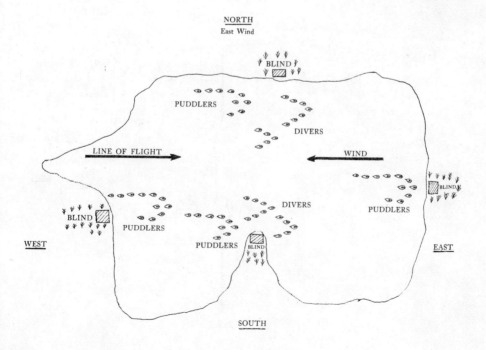

NORTH
East Wind

BLIND

PUDDLERS

DIVERS

LINE OF FLIGHT WIND

BLIND

DIVERS

BLIND PUDDLERS

WEST BLIND PUDDLERS EAST

PUDDLERS BLIND

SOUTH

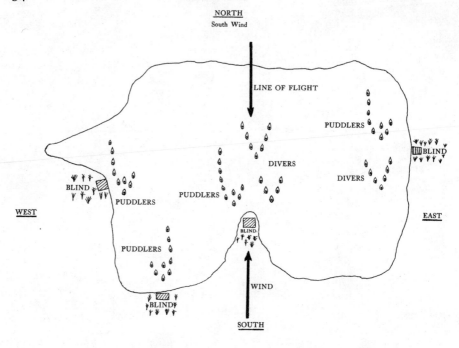

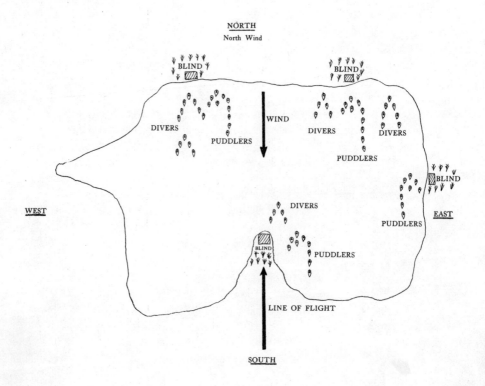

7

Decoy Attitudes

Many, many years ago I tumbled ducks over rigs consisting of quart-size tin cans painted gray and black and oblong slabs of cork. And I killed ducks; sometimes limits.

These "poor boy" rigs worked because ducks were fairly plentiful then and because I gunned areas most hunters considered to be inaccessible. The places were "off limits," so to speak, simply because so many waterfowlers felt that to trudge so deep into the marshes was too much work. These same "poor boy" decoys will work today if a hunter can find a place where birds are numerous and there is very little competition from other hunters. This, indeed, is a rare combination now.

The illegitimate replicas didn't pull ducks in to give me true decoying shots. Almost all shots were pass ones snapped off in a hurry at birds curious enough to buzz the spread for a closer look. I can't recall having anything other than an occasional shoveller or redhead actually drop into the water with this rig. Even though this kind of shooting was satisfying at the time, I now look back at it with regrets. How I wish I had owned real decoys. Ducks working to decoys are poetry in motion. It's a thrilling sight to behold—even if it is culminated in three shots and three complete misses.

The point is ducks will vector in for a closer look at a lot of things that from a distance may resemble other ducks on the water. There is, however, a big difference between a duck just looking and one actually bent on decoying. The resulting shots are poles apart.

Not only are duck populations down from decades ago, but today the army of hunters has increased many fold. Except for ultra-exclusive hunting clubs owning or leasing vast acreage and the few hard-to-reach places left, the bulk of the natural duck habitat areas are hunted quite heavily. This extra gun pressure only makes the birds skitterish and hard to decoy.

The waterfowler, if he is to be consistently successful, must use decoys that look like and act like the duck species sought. A decoy to be effective must have more duck-like qualities than merely a duck shape and authentic coloring. Its attitude on calm water and then how it rides choppy water are important. The position of the head is extremely important.

Let's start with decoys before they are ever placed on the water. An erect neck with the head held high may appeal to the eye of the hunter. Not so with real ducks. A duck holds its neck and head in this attitude when it is walking. Swimming on a pond, a peaceful duck will nestle its head well down on its shoulders. A swimming duck when nervous, frightened and about ready to fly holds its neck erect and head high. So what is the point of using decoys that are perfect imitations of scared ducks? A rig of such blocks will pull in some ducks, but it will spook many times more.

Puddle ducks—mallards, black ducks, gadwalls, teal and so forth—ride high on the water. Their tail feathers sweep upward distinctively. Diving ducks like canvasbacks, bluebills and redheads ride low and deep in the water with their tails slanted downward or at least parallel to the surface of the water.

If your puddler decoy rides like a diver or vice versa, the best advice to follow is to simply refinish them to resemble the duck species they closest imitate in attitude on the water.

A decoy that can be deadly on a calm pond can become a bird-spooker on rough water. Ducks always ride the water into the wind. This means the duck also rides facing the chop. Ducks will bob up and down in rough water, but they do not roll from side to side like a barroom habitue. Any decoy that rolls from side to side should never be used in heavy seas.

A clue to the decoy's performance in rough water can be gleaned by noting the shape of its bottom. Those with rounded bottoms are likely to roll violently in a chop. Decoys with flat bottoms maintain proper attitude. Flat bottom blocks, however, require a deeper keel for quicker righting in the event they turn over.

Long anchor lines are necessary in rough water even though a short line may hold the decoy in place. The short line is likely to cause the decoy to dig into wavelets instead of riding over them. Real ducks ride over the chop; they never bore right through it.

Most commercial decoys today have eyelets or rings fore and aft for attaching anchor lines. It beats me why some hunters keep insisting on using the rear-end hook up. Ducks always—but always—ride into the wind wind. Why louse it all up by setting out decoys with their tails to the wind? If there is a complete absence of wind and

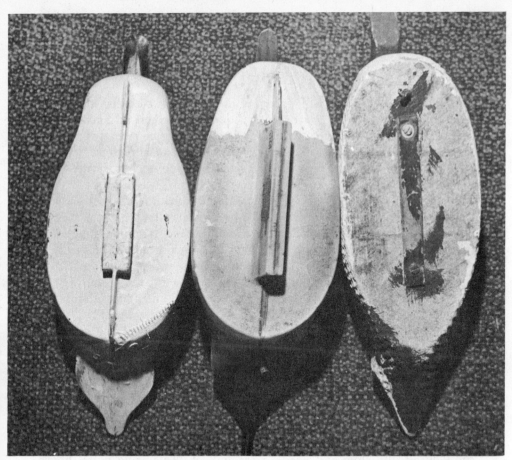

Keels are the keys as to how decoys will act on the water. Large and deep keels on plastic decoys (left and center) will keep blocks upright in rough water. Lead strip on wooden decoy (right) is insufficient to keep it from rolling from side to side in rough water.

This is view from a blind of puddle decoy rig set for shooting in a cross wind. Enough decoys must be placed out to be conspicuous on the water, yet adequate open space must be left for decoying birds.

water currents, ducks will face in all directions. Under the same conditions decoys will face in all directions even when all anchor lines are attached to the bow rings. There is absolutely no need for rigging anchor lines to the rear of decoys, unless a second and third decoy is strung in line with the first. In this case a single anchor secures two or more blocks.

A properly set rig can be ruined if the anchors fail to hold and blocks drift out of position. Some waterfowlers seek to whip this by increasing the weight of anchors. Personally I feel it can be done more effectively by increasing the length of the anchor line. Decoys held by short lines will stay put but lengthier lines will permit the blocks to tack back and forth in the wind. This motion adds realism.

To paraphrase an old saying, the anchor line itself should be "felt and not seen." It is felt in that it holds the blocks in place. Under no circumstances should it be visible to flying birds. Use lines that match the color of the water and make sure these lines sink. Set decoys out so the anchor lines run from the connection ring or post on the bottom of the block. Never allow lines to loop around necks or over bills.

Properly constructed decoys are ballasted to ride upright. The weight must be sufficient for the block to quickly right itself if it is inadvertently tipped over. Any decoy that comes back to the upright in a dreadfully slow roll needs extra ballast. An upside down block, particularly if it is on the rig perimeter, will spook a flock of decoying birds. Furthermore the decoy that rights itself in slow motion is a cinch to be the one that rolls from side to side in rough water.

Some makes of decoys are without keels and are ballasted with weights inside their bodies. Personally I prefer those with keels. Blocks without keels tend to ride rather static. Those with keels zig zag back and forth, and action in decoys is like action in fishing lures—positive results are obtained.

Waterlogging is a problem with wooden decoys. Any waterlogged puddler decoys should be set on the shoreline to mimic feeders or sleepers. When diver blocks became waterlogged and ride so low that water washes over their backs, it's time to give them a rest. A half-sunk decoy is worse than one that has its head or bill knocked off.

The fellow owning decoys with movable heads should make the most of this versatility. Turn the heads in different directions. On a windless day, when decoys face in all directions, you might even turn a few heads completely around to convert the blocks into sleepers. But never rig sleepers in a formation—V or fish hook—when the whole purpose of the pattern is to give flying birds the impression that the blocks on the water are swimming some place. Ducks just don't swim and sleep simultaneously.

From a side view a decoy's bill should be either slanted slightly

A pair of "showboat" decoys made by the author. Mallard hen is in front. Decoy in back is that of hen black duck.

down toward the water or at least be parallel with the surface. A bill that points skyward, even at a slight angle, belongs to a nervous duck that is about ready to take wing for more comfortable surroundings.

In the more frigid range of duck habitat, waterfowlers may at times be faced with hunting in freezing weather. Nothing looks worse than a spread of decoys with icicles hanging from their bills. This can spook nervous birds and prolong the hunter's agony in a frigid blind. The hard way to remedy the situation is to wade out to knock off the icicles. An easier way is to take a preventive step back at home: melt some wax and then with a brush stroke it on the bills. After it hardens moisture that used to collect on the bill will run off like the water off the proverbial duck's back.

I tried this same stunt by coating bills with a light film of oil. Results were disastrous. The bills shed water, but every time a wavelet dashed against them, oil washed off, stained the water and made the pond glisten like a rainbow. And, of course, ducks that may have decoyed shied off for parts unknown. Anyway the only way to learn some things is by making mistakes.

In the case of puddle ducks you really don't need water deep enough for the decoys to float. Just set them out firmly so they remain upright. Keep in mind that if the wind tips this decoy over, the ballast weight will not bring it back to upright position. By all means arrange a few blocks around clumps of vegetation that may show. Make them look like feeders. You might even put a few right in the

More of the author's "showboat" decoys. This much detail on hens is not necessary if blocks are located in the center of the rig. "Showboat" blocks should be placed on perimeter of the rig. The drake mallard "sleeper" should be used near the shoreline. No eyes are needed on "sleeper" decoys.

clumps of grass. Ducks like to climb up and rest on these little mounds. All of these little realistic touches help, especially so when the ducks are already skitterish because of hunting pressure in the area.

The placement of males and females is not to be overlooked. Never group all the drakes in one place and the hens in another. Intermingle but intermingle them the way real ducks do. Hens generally tend to work closer to the shoreline than do the drakes. More drakes than hens prefer to congregate near the head of a spread, although early in the season the lead duck on the water is likely to be a hen. In late December and early January, especially if the weather is warm, the drakes appear to get the "pairing off" urge and begin to show aggressiveness by taking the lead on the water.

All of these things may appear to be little, but I look at it this way—a lot of little drops can make a full glass of wine. Anything that tends to pull birds into easy gun range is worth pursuing.

The hunter who has several blinds at his disposal should make the most of this option in relation to existing light conditions.

The ideal shooting situation is to have the wind blowing from behind the blind. This makes decoying birds come in from dead ahead, but this can be tough on the hunter's eyes if he is shooting into the sun. The waterfowler will enjoy his shoot more by switching to another blind where he won't be facing directly into the sun. Instead of head-on shots, he will get birds working across from one side or the other.

A duck coming out of the sun has two advantages over the hunter. First and most obvious the hunter is likely to miss seeing the bird until too late. The second duck advantage has to do with the decoys themselves. That sun is going to spotlight them, and every phony color, shine or whatnot will stick out like a fly in the cup of coffee. Even flat paints will glisten a bit in strong sunlight, and it may be enough to make birds vector away. At best the hunter's shots will be at long range.

Even if it means shooting at an angle, it pays in the long run to spread the rig so that decoying birds will work into the sun. You can see their approach much easier. Furthermore they approach the decoys from the "shadow side." Thus any blocks with obvious flaws won't stand out like a ballerina in the spotlight.

8

Number of Decoys

The waterfowler can use a half dozen decoys in one area and bag easy limits of ducks, whereas in another area he may need several dozen blocks to even get birds to give his spread a passing flight of inquiry.

The number of decoys to use depends upon (1) species of ducks sought, (2) size of water area gunned, (3) hunting pressure in the immediate area, and (4) visibility.

Again going back to the characteristics of species we find that puddler ducks are more susceptible to stooling to a small rig than are divers. During the course of migration travels all species of ducks tend to move in concentrations that number into hundreds of birds. But once they reach wintering grounds, they again break up into small flocks. The size of these small flocks will depend upon the duck species.

Most puddlers—like mallards, black ducks, gadwalls, and blue-winged teal—tend to break into flocks of a dozen or less birds. Exceptions are the pintail and the green-winged teal. These species are more likely to be found in flocks numbering many dozen. Green-wings, however, will break into quite small bunches when they get into marsh country where there are a great many small ponds and potholes.

Like the puddlers divers migrate in large concentrations, but upon reaching wintering grounds these big masses break up. The groups, however, are not nearly so small as their puddler counterparts. Diver groups in wintering areas are likely to be in groups numbering scores of birds.

When flights are large, a small decoy spread is not going to

62

produce much action. Rarely will the hunter experience days when a flock of 30 or 40 birds will decoy to a spread of a half dozen to a dozen blocks. Old market hunters used to say that if the flying bunch numbers two more birds than the blocks on the water, the birds won't work to the rig. Personally I don't feel the rule is that rigid, and I am inclined to amend it to flights a time and a half as numerous as the decoys. Still I have had this shot full of holes by having 30 or so green-winged teal pitch in with a spread of a dozen decoys. This, however, is an extreme rarity when mallards, black ducks, pintails, gadwalls and baldpates are concerned. It also holds true for the diving ducks, although bluebills have a tendency to sometimes stool to spreads that contain few decoys.

Three dozen blocks on a pond 50 feet in diameter are too many. This many decoys doesn't leave much open water to which the birds can work. A dozen blocks would do the job better as long as they were models of puddle ducks. The puddlers will work to such small ponds; divers will not.

The spread with three dozen blocks works well on expansive bodies of water, and such a rig—one with even more decoys—may

The right amount of decoys for shooting on a small pond. Never over-crowd water with decoys. These 16 plastic decoys when deflated can be carried easily in a tow sack.

be necessary even though the flights are small in number. The problem here is to have enough decoys to show up, for the larger the body of water the more likely the blocks will be missed. From a quarter mile away a spread of three dozen blocks shows up much better than just a dozen. And five dozen will do a better job than three dozen.

Big spreads are absolute musts when the water is rough, for when, as often happens, decoys are in the troughs between waves, low flying birds are not likely to see them. I've had times when I needed six to seven dozen blocks on the water to pull birds close enough for effective shooting. Yet in the same area on the very next day on calm water a rig of two dozen would pull birds much better.

In areas where there is heavy hunting pressure, big spreads of decoys are necessary. This holds true for both puddlers and divers.

A lot of decoys, especially showy ones, are needed when visibility is poor due to fog, mist or rain. By showy blocks, I mean drakes of the species. They are more brightly colored than the hens and are likely to appear as more than just an indistinct blob on the water. These showy decoys have a visibility advantage on rough water, too.

On bright days when you can see to the horizon and then some, a spread with a generous sprinkling of hens is quite effective. A good drake to hen ratio is two to one.

Most commercial decoys today are oversize—but just slightly. In recent years there has been a marked trend toward the manufacture of even larger oversize blocks. Experienced waterfowlers view these time and a half to twice as large blocks with mixed feelings—usually disdain or unemotional resignation. I have met few real dyed-in-the-wool duck hunters who waxed enthusiastic over the behemoths.

Personally I feel there are a few situations that may call for use of oversize blocks. These include shooting over rough water where many decoys are likely to be out of sight when they ride down into the troughs, and on foggy days. But on a bright day or in rain—no! Why? Simply because their size is out of character with their sur-roundings on a clear day. Most modern oversize blocks are made of plastic, and in a rain they glisten far more than the realistically smaller decoys.

The waterfowler bent on using huge oversize decoys would be better off to skip the biggie duck species and go with a few full-bodied, full-size goose decoys. Two or three would be sufficient to augment the duck spread of a dozen blocks. A half dozen goose decoys would be sufficient for the duck rig with three or four dozen blocks.

The presence of geese always serves to allay any nervousness the flying ducks may have. Geese just don't stay on the ground or water when there is danger around. They are wary, suspicious birds that case a place thoroughly before cupping wings to set. Apparently ducks are fully cognizant of this fact.

Use of goose decoys to supplement the duck rig requires care in where they are spotted. Never place them at the head of a spread. From the middle of the rig back, group the goose blocks off to one side. If shore vegetation is high, the goose blocks should be placed on the outside of the duck spread. Geese do not like their 360 degree visibility hindered. Goose blocks placed two or three yards out from shoreline vegetation that stands 10 feet tall is completely out of character. But if the shoreline vegetation is low and sparse, place the goose blocks between the duck rig and the shoreline. You might even put several right up on land, for geese are very likely to move out of the water to feed on the shoreline and up in the short grass proper.

In selecting goose decoys for this purpose, pay particular attention to neck and head attitudes. Don't get models that all have their necks and heads upright. Purchase some with turned-down necks and heads to simulate feeders. The goose blocks can be any of three species— Canada, snow or blue. The snows and blues because of the large areas of white on their bodies are visible from considerable distances. They can be real Jim Dandies when visibility is low.

It's just a matter of taste, but personally I dislike shooting over spreads with huge numbers of decoys. Three, four or five dozen is enough. Those two and three hundred block spreads are a heck of a lot of work to set out for the small bag limits we have today. It takes just as much work to gather them up after a hunt, and then there is the portage problem.

I have a second reason for disliking huge spreads. If the blocks are spotted so there is open water between the blind and the spread— and this is necessary to get the birds close—a great many decoys on the outer perimeter may be out of range. You'll get birds with this rig, but you'll also have a lot of headaches. Cripples will invariably fall in among the blocks. I've seen dogs go out for these birds, get tangled in decoy anchor lines and then lose the cripple to boot.

If you don't have a dog, this means having to finish the cripples on the water before they swim out of range. Ever try to pop a cripple in the decoys and still not shotriddle the blocks? The results are disaster if inflatable decoys are used. Molded plastic decoys will be shot-punctured, usually around the waterline, and this means a sinker. It's common to have shot knock heads and bills completely off wooden blocks.

Some waterfowlers in using this multi-hundred spread try to beat this by grouping the blocks in close to the blind, leaving no open water between rig and blind or shoreline. At least this will keep all blocks within gun range. But how about the ducks? They are certain to work to the outside of the rig, usually in extreme range. Consequently there will be a lot of long range shots and lost cripples. Every cripple lost is one less to breed and maintain population levels for future seasons. Look at it this way. If the cripple that escaped is a drake, the loss is one bird. But if the lost bird is a hen, then the loss is closer to six birds—the hen and the brood she would have raised the following spring on the nesting grounds.

Hunters don't stop hunting until they have the limit in hand. I have no figures on the national loss average in cripples, but one year in Texas in a state-regulated marsh the loss was 28 percent. Suppose the daily limit is four birds and two hunters go out. The odds are they will have to knock down 10 birds in order to retrieve eight. Suppose the 10 birds dropped included five hens. Using actuary calculations one could say the two hunters trimmed the actual duck population by ten but the future population by 35 birds. And then we don't know how many birds seemingly missed were actually hit, flew on a mile or so and then fell dead. These two hunters could actually have sliced 50 birds from the future duck population.

The sole purpose of decoys is to lure birds within range for effective shooting. It is poor conservation to compromise the whole purpose of the rig in forcing the birds to work at long range where cripple losses are certain to be high. Back when duck shooting was unrestricted, the old market hunters didn't waste shells on long shots. They set their decoys so the birds would come in close. They wanted every shell to count because every miss cost them money.

Shooting the same pond day in and day out is certainly not recommended. You will enjoy fine shooting the first week, but after that the hunting will taper off sharply. What happens is that the ducks quickly learn to avoid those ponds that daily spit lead at them.

Yet there may be situations when one pond and one pond only is available to a fellow. If he insists on hunting it daily, he should be willing to make day to day alterations in his decoy rig. Vary the number of decoys used. Vary the rig formation from V to fish hook to cluster. The hunter who owns two or more species of decoys can take still another step. For example, put out only mallards one day and only pintails the next. This day-by-day alternation will to some extent help in overcoming gunshyness on the part of local ducks.

Regardless what formation is used, how many decoys are used or what the decoy species may be, don't leave the blocks on the pond overnight or for days at a time. This may eliminate a lot of repetitious work of taking in and setting out blocks, but it also curtails hunter success. Ducks often move around at night, especially when the moon is full and bright. It doesn't take them long to learn that decoys are harbingers of sudden departure from this world, and they act accordingly to those ponds from which decoys are never removed. Man may have the superior brain, but we must never assume that ducks are stupid. They, too, can think and learn, although of course on a less sophisticated level than man.

I can name a dozen waterfowlers who can list another reason for not leaving decoys unattended on the pond. The blocks may not be able to fly; nevertheless they are spirited away in the black of night. I know one fellow who had a rig of 60 plastic decoys vanish from a ten-acre lake. The "spirits" that copped those blocks had to walk in a mile to do it. The gate was still locked and there were no fresh car tracks on the muddy road.

9

The "Confidence" Game

Read literature on oldtime waterfowling and you will find frequent mention of the "confidence" decoy. This was the decoy set out to give flying birds the impression that the area below them was a place of safety.

In early decoy shooting the confidence decoys were invariably of waterfowl species not normally hunted. Up the Atlantic seaboard various species of gulls were staked out as the confidence decoys. Apparently there was some merit in the system because a great many waterfowlers used them.

Until 1935, when live decoys were outlawed, many shooters looked to these in the light of confidence birds. In this case they depended more on the quacking and chattering of the live birds to lure in ducks than on whatever motions the birds themselves might make.

Today the confidence block is seldom used the way it was by early waterfowlers. I feel this is perhaps due to a change in the shooting habits of modern hunters. Early waterfowlers carefully husbanded powder and shot. They held off blasting away until the bird was well within range. Furthermore they could tell at a glance a duck from a sea gull, tern or other species of shorebird. Today's hunters fire shells like they were going out of style. Not only that, they go afield totally unprepared when it comes to duck identification. An appalling number shoot at anything and everything that flies. They are able to identify it as a duck only when the bird is in hand. Consequently protected gulls, terns and hawks are clobbered in the process. With this kind of shooting there are no birds left around in which a poor duck can put its trust.

It's the American way to gripe and then do nothing about it. This

*When all is right on a pond, ducks waste little time in getting down to feeding.
The ducks above are shovellers. Feeding ducks always give confidence to
decoying birds.*

*These coot are in a playful mood racing up and down a small lake. They
make excellent confidence birds for diving ducks like redheads and bluebills
and puddle duck species like baldpates and shovellers.*

attitude is the reason we have short waterfowl seasons and small bag limits. If hunters could learn to identify before they shoot and then act accordingly, we could all get more enjoyment out of the sport. But as long as guys shoot at anything that flies, we can expect to feel the pinch of regulations. Again why should a poor duck put its trust in other birds that are subjected to indiscriminate shooting?

The most common confidence decoys used today are ducks—or rather ducks posed in certain attitudes. These are the "feeder" and "sleeper" blocks. Their purpose is not basically to attract ducks to the area, but rather one of allaying suspicion. They should be used in conjunction with decoys in normal swimming poses.

The "sleeper" is the more common of the two. This decoy has its head snuggled well down on its body or turned so it rests on the back. The decoy with its head turned on its back can also be called a preening block. It's a good one to use, for ducks don't go around preening their feathers if they are alerted to danger in the immediate area.

Care, however, must be taken as to when and where to use the "sleepers" and "preeners." Ducks sleep and preen only in sheltered waters; they do neither on rough seas. I find it pointless to use either when hunting in a howling norther.

There are two types of feeder decoys. One simply has its front end shaped off to give the impression that the duck has its head stuck underwater. There is no head whatsoever on this block. The other is really half a decoy—the rear end. This sticks straight up in the air to imitate a duck that has "tipped" the entire front portion of its body underwater. Again one must know when and where to use these "feeders."

The first "feeder" block described can be used in fairly choppy water. The second must be used only in calm water, for a chop will make the "tipper" pendulum unnaturally.

There is no question about "feeders" and "sleepers" being confidence decoys. They signal to flying birds that all is well and to come down to join the party. The "feeders" are particularly effective when used in areas where natural duck fodder is scarce. Ducks fly for two reasons. One is to find a suitable resting area. The other is to find food. When food is abundant throughout an area, ducks are less likely to pay heed to "feeder" decoys.

I have found "sleeper" blocks deadly rascals in heavily hunted areas. In this situation flying birds are constantly being chased by shot, and their goal is to find a place where they can catch a quick nap.

On one occasion my hunting partner and I split for our morning shoot. Inadvertently he took the sack of decoys containing blocks imitating swimmers. I was left with a sack of "sleepers." Our hunting ponds were about 300 yards apart and in a natural local flyway. The

The snowy egret makes a wonderful confidence bird. When these birds come near blind or decoys, they should be allowed to remain. These birds are on the protected list and should not be shot. The above egret is beside a box blind.

marsh was also gunned quite frequently so the birds were naturally leery. Ducks that passed his decoy spread doing a mile a minute circled in beautifully to my "sleepers." I got all the shooting that morning.

Don't jump to the conclusion that an all-"sleeper" spread is the perfect spread. Just keep in mind that all birds in a flock will not be sleeping at the same time. This only happens in the zoo where the birds are tame and know they are safe from predators. In the wild there will always be a few birds alert and ready to give alarm if danger arises. A pair of "sleepers" in every dozen decoys is a good ratio to maintain.

Personally the best all around confidence decoy is the goose. Any duck spread augmented with a few goose decoys will pull birds. Geese are wary birds that just won't set unless the coast is clear. Ducks seem to know this, and they respond accordingly.

During the course of a hunt a variety of birds other than ducks will circle and may light in the vicinity of the decoys. These live fellows, whether they are seagulls, curlews, or common blackbirds, lend an air of authenticity to the surroundings. Don't chase them away; let them stay. But just don't become so engrossed in watching their proceedings as to miss seeing incoming ducks. It can happen. A couple of seasons back I had a flight of long-billed curlews land on the shoreline near my decoys. The hunting had been slow to start off with and with nothing flying it was only natural for me to watch

The above pond is obviously a peaceful one with its array of shorebirds. The pond included a number of ducks but they were hidden from view by marsh grass in foreground.

the curlews stick their long curved bills deep into the mud for choice tidbits. After a while I stood up in the blind to stretch my legs.

"Kaack, kaack, kaack." The sudden squawking of two hen mallards leaping off the water almost made me jump out of my boots. And, of course, they were specks on the horizon before I could get my gun. I never did see the birds decoy; I had been too interested in the feeding curlews. And to make matters worse not another duck flew that morning.

There is one bird that should be driven away if it flies in the vicinity of the decoys. It's the hawk—any species. Ducks just will not fly near a place where hawks are circling. But scare the hawk away; don't shoot it. These birds of prey are beneficial in controlling the rodent population.

10
The Geese

Geese are waterfowl that spend more time on land than on water. Except for a few species of sea geese, these big birds roost, feed and rest on land. They have excellent mobility on land, and on typical rough prairie or marsh terrain a mature goose can outrun a man. The legs of geese are so located that the birds are well balanced. They can run, make sharp turns and relatively sudden stops without falling down or tumbling end over end. None of the duck species have such good balance.

Geese will go to water at least once, sometimes twice, each day. The visits are usually short, just long enough to drink and dabble a bit. Whenever geese spend a lot of their time out on the water, it is because they are suspicious and untrusting of something on the shore or in the fields. In areas where wild rice and wild celery abound, geese are likely to do considerable feeding in shallow water.

Ducks frequently move into an area, and if the food supply is bountiful and there is nothing to alarm the birds, the quackers may remain for days on end. I have seen wild ducks, especially mallards, spend a full week on a choice pond without so much as flying out of the area a single time. You won't find this true of geese, for they rarely roost and feed on the same area. Although ducks, and again especially so with mallards, often will feed to a point where they seemingly have difficulty flying, they do not strip an area bare of all edible vegetation. Geese are voracious feeders. A big concentration of geese can strip a field as bare as a soup bone after a hound dog is through with it. Furthermore these big birds can bare a field in the space of a few days. After the spilled grain is gone, they go for the tender emergent vegetation. If the overall general area is hard put for fodder, these geese will next start "rooting," burrowing their bills into the soil to dig out the roots. In short, if there is nothing to molest the birds or drive them from the area, they can turn a field to bare earth.

Whether on breeding grounds in the spring and summer or on wintering grounds through the fall and winter months, geese tend to use the same roosts day after day. These birds usually feed twice a day. Sometimes they fly back to the roosting area between feeding sessions, but more often they fly into a resting area, usually located between the roost and feeding area. Since these birds can clean out a feed area so effectively, it should be obvious that the longer the geese are in an area, the longer their feed flights will become as nearby fields are laid barren. It is not uncommon for geese to pick up and wing 10 to 20 miles to some choice grain field or pea patch.

Their normal everyday habit is to leave the roost about a half hour to an hour after sunrise to wing to feeding grounds. If the feeding grounds are completely barren of water, the birds will break their feeding session with a flight to water. After they have fed and

When waterfowl move in huge concentrations like these snow geese, large numbers of decoys are necessary to attract the birds. (Photo courtesy Galveston Convention and Tourist Bureau.)

watered to capacity they fly to a rest area, which can be the roost if it is nearby. The feed and water routine is repeated again late in the afternoon, and then shortly before sunset the birds wing to the roost.

It behooves the goose hunter to study the local flights. The first thing to locate is the roost, and then follow the flight of the birds from there. Under no circumstances hunt the roost itself. It is okay to get a quarter mile or so from the roost and either hunt the birds over decoys or pass shooting as they leave or return to the roost. But to sneak right into the concentration and gun the roost proper only chases the game completely out of the area. The old market hunters used to do it this way and they called it "busting a roost." Their method was to sneak in at night when the birds had only a minimum of sentinels posted. The market gunners raked the birds on the ground and killed great numbers of them. The shooting, of course, put the concentration to wing, but the market hunters could have cared less for shooting the birds on the ground assured them of big kills. It mattered not to them that the birds would completely quit a roost area after a couple of "bustings."

It is far easier to hunt geese on land than it is on water. Canada geese and sub-species of the Canada can be hunted successfully and consistently on water, but when it comes to such species as speckle-bellies, snows and blues, the best hunting is usually on land. These three species will work well to decoys spotted on land, but only with some reluctance will they stool to decoys on water. In fact, the speckle-belly shows a distinct distaste for flying low over water. In lake country this goose will fly a meandering path to stay over land masses when moving from roost to feeding area and vice versa. This is true on short flights of just a few miles or so when the birds are likely to fly quite low. On long migrations and when the birds climb to altitudes of many thousand feet, they show no hesitation about flying over water. When these birds go to water, they show a decided preference in setting down on land near the shoreline and then trooping to the water. Snow and blue geese show this same tendency but to a lesser degree.

Actually many geese bagged over water are shot incidental to duck hunting when the waterfowler puts out a decoy spread primarily for ducks and supplements it with a few goose decoys as extra lures just in case some geese happen to fly in the area. Canada geese and sub-species will descend in number to a good goose spread on water. In the case of snow and blue geese, it is rare for more than one or two birds to work to a goose decoy rig on the water. Usually those that work are juveniles that have been separated from their parents.

All geese show a marked dislike either of flying low over or setting down near growths or structures that project appreciably above the surface. In over-water shooting, the hunting blind built on stilts

A characteristic of snow and blue geese on wintering grounds is their love of company. A large flight is shown decoying. Birds on ground have just landed and all have necks and heads raised to survey surroundings. After they found no danger lurking, they started to feed.

is certain to fall into this category. Hence geese often shy away from decoys on the water because of the blind itself and particularly so if the hunting pressure is heavy in the general area.

The hunter who seeks his geese on land will have far better opportunities to hide himself than the fellow who tries for his game over water. The land hunter does not have to resort to blinds that stand noticeably above ground level.

Yet because of the characteristics and suspicious nature of geese any old place on land won't suffice. The area must be reasonably open, for when geese are on the ground, they want to be able to eyeball 360 degrees. They do not like to fly low over trees, tall brush, buildings and particularly improved roads. They will cross a prairie or marsh at an altitude of a hundred or so feet and cross dirt roads without increasing altitude. But just let that prairie or marsh be sliced by a hard-topped road, and even when there is no traffic on the road, birds approaching it will start increasing their altitude when they are several hundred yards from it. By the time they cross the road, they are usually well above shotgun range. Then several hundred yards on the other side of the road they begin a gradual descent to their original altitude. They do the same thing when buildings, trees, thick fence rows and hills are involved. Interestingly enough these same birds increase altitude just enough to clear powerlines that may bisect a marsh or prairie.

In the case of buildings, clumps of trees, a windmill or a large mound, Canada geese and sub-species as well as speckle-belly geese tend strongly to meander around rather than fly over. Snow and blue geese are inclined to beat a more direct path and simply climb higher to maintain a safe distance.

Keeping in mind that these birds always decoy into the wind, the hunter should locate well downwind of any obstructions or buildings. A gunner too close to these uprisings is going to find himself faced with a lot of extremely long range shots. If circumstances force a gunner to spread his decoys upwind of the trees, ridge or what have you, he should stay at least 300 yards away. Under normal conditions this is sufficient to allow the birds to descend back to their original altitude. In areas where the hunting pressure is heavy it is not uncommon for geese to add altitude upon approach to each obstacle and then maintain that increase in height after passing it. This, however, is most likely to occur on days when skies are clear and there is little wind. It is a different story when the wind has some muscle in it, for then the birds will pick the most opportune height at which to fly. Wind velocity on any given day will vary at different heights, and usually the stronger the wind, the lower the geese fly. To some degree the contour of the land, the trees, buildings and ridges cause variances in wind velocity. The geese fathom these changes and seek them out for the easiest flying.

If a goose hunter is to be successful, he must hide his presence from approaching birds. Naturally one's thoughts turn immediately to the terrain and how it can be used advantageously. Let's take a hypothetical situation. The hunting area between roost and feeding grounds is an expansive prairie. Its flatness is broken by a few lonesome wind-blown and wind-stunted trees, some scraggly bushes and stands of waist-high grass. In addition there are a few marshy depressions, a dirt road bordered by poor excuses for ditches and several transects of barbed wire fences. What makes good cover and what makes poor cover for the goose hunter?

Those lonesome trees and bushes are the worst places to seek cover. They may effectively screen you from the birds, but because they stand out and break the flatness of the terrain, the geese will either tower to go over them or meander around. Either way the game will very likely be out of range. Those stands of waist-high grass will suffice unless the overall area is hunted hard. In this case the geese will tend to go over high or skirt around the edges. Those marshy depressions and the ditches bordering the dirt road will make

Geese don't like to fly low over any objects that may hide enemies. Note these snow and blue geese are crossing from one field to another but they are crossing in an opening between the trees.

excellent hides if the hunter wears camouflaged clothes, keeps his head down and remains still. If the marshy depressions fill with water in wet weather, one can expect speckle-belly geese to react accordingly and fly around, rather than over them.

There is not much to an individual post in a barbed wire fence, yet as slim as it may be, it offers fine opportunities for the goose hunter. For some reason geese come to accept such things as fences and tend to fly right over them without putting on any altitude. With a good spread of decoys around him, the hunter hunkering behind a fence post can get some fine shooting if the geese involved are snows or blues.

Geese are mainly vegetarians, feeding on grain, berries, grass and marsh growths, but unlike ducks they feed with considerable caution. A stealthy hunter can sneak into gun range of feeding ducks, but it is not likely that he will be able to do the same thing with geese. Two special traits hold the answer.

Number one, geese never like to land either on water or land if surrounding vegetation is so tall that they cannot eyeball the horizon in all directions. Number two, every gaggle of geese—whether on land or water—has a few watch ganders on sentry duty. These sentinel birds on water sit off from the flock or on land find a slight rise in the ground and stand atop it. While the other birds feed or rest, the watch ganders keep their necks stretched and heads high to eagle-eye the area. If something suspicious occurs, the watch ganders give the alarm and the entire flock takes to wing. The same birds don't stand watch duty all day. The sentries change like the palace guard, with the new watchers taking a station almost identical to that of the birds they relieve. The watch ganders are invariably old birds. Geese are very intelligent birds, and they don't risk important watch missions to inexperienced juveniles.

Geese mate for life and have very strong family ties. This year's hatch will stay with the parents until the clan returns north to breed next spring. Then the year old birds strike off to mate and raise families of their own. Geese migrate in huge concentrations and at high altitudes. Airline pilots have reported encountering migrating geese at altitudes of 10,000 feet. Their migration flights are in the distinctive V formations, but unlike ducks, they make a lot of noise when flying. Geese are constantly talking while in flight, whereas ducks are almost always silent. Flying ducks will start a little talking when they begin to decoy, but even here the talk is rather subdued. Ducks do all their chattering when they are on the land or water.

After geese reach their wintering grounds, the big concentrations tend to break back into small family groups. This is more pronounced with the Canada goose and its sub-species; snows and blues tend to hold together in considerable concentrations. Consequently it is easier to pull the Canadas to a small spread of decoys than it is with the snows and blues.

Geese, especially snows and blues, fly locally much higher than ducks, and this altitude is in direct relation to the wind and weather. The clearer the skies and the less the wind velocity, the higher the birds are likely to fly. Unless the birds are bent on flying many miles, these local flights take no definite formation but fall more into irregular groups. Whenever the waterfowler sees flying geese in a definite formation, he can pretty well bet they are not going to have any truck with his spread of decoys.

Geese are like ducks in that they approach a landing spot from downwind. Their approach, however, is much slower, and in the case of the Canadas it is likely to take a weaving back and forth pattern. Sometimes this approach follows the contour of the land with the birds flying over the ridges. Geese tend less to circle and figure-eight over a landing area as is so common with ducks in the puddler group.

11

Goose Spreads

The effectiveness of a goose decoy rig depends on three things: (1) number of decoys, (2) relationship of the rig to the wind, and (3) spacing of the individual decoys. The number of decoys needed and rig relationship to wind were discussed in preceding chapters, and there is no point of repetition here other than to remind that decoys should always face or quarter into the wind.

Now to that all important spacing. Always keep in mind that waterfowl, whether they are ducks or geese, tend to bunch up when suspicious or nervous. This is an impression you don't want your spread to give. You want your rig to indicate that all is cozy and that here is a fine place for other birds to gather to feed, gab or rest. This illusion can only be accomplished by keeping the decoys spread out. The general spacing for duck decoys on water is about five feet between blocks. In the case of geese the distance between blocks should be about double that of ducks, whether the spread is spotted on land or water.

The importance of this can be understood if you study geese taking to the air. Study individual birds as well as gaggle action. The most apparent thing is the great wingspan of these birds—4½ to 5 feet for snows and blues and up to 6 feet for Canada honkers. This means the birds need considerable distance between each other to prevent mid-air collisions. These birds have powerful wing beats, and this is most evident when they arise from a dry field. A big concentration of geese taking off can stir up dust like a helicopter. The powerful wing beats create air swirls and eddies that can make balance unstable for other birds that may be extremely close.

All species of geese migrate in large concentrations that may include several hundred families, but after they reach their wintering

These hunters are heading for a goose shoot in a plowed field. One hunter carries a sack of full-bodied decoys, while the second drags a bundle of white plastic jugs. The jugs aid in making a big "show of white" in the field.

Hunter in white cape and coveralls sits in middle of white rag spread for snow geese. This type of spread is popular and very effective in Texas goose country.

grounds, most species tend to break back down to single family or two to three family units. Only the Canada goose and its sub-species tend to stick to one family units on wintering grounds, and about the only time several of these families unite is when the flight from roost to feeding grounds and vice versa covers many miles. Then a number of families may wing together, since this kind of traveling is easier on all the birds involved. The lead goose breaks the trail so to speak, and the following geese ride the vortices created by the strong wing beats of the birds immediately ahead. When the lead goose tires, another adult takes over. Hence a lengthy local flight is made easiest when several families pool their energies and leadership is shared by several adults.

Again when geese alight either to feed, rest or roost, they tend to drift apart and cluster in single family groups. Observe closely a big concentration on the ground. It may number many hundreds of birds, and at a quick glance appear to be a solid mass. But upon close examination one will note the mass is made up of a lot of groups composed of from three to eight or nine birds. View such a concentration from a high angle and these small groups are easily distinguishable. Only when the birds are alarmed or suspicious will the families move in close to tighten the concentration. Even then they do not move in so close that they have no takeoff or flying room.

The many family groups vs. the single big concentration aspects of geese may be kept in mind when spotting a decoy rig. A big rig with decoys placed close together will pull flying birds over for a look-see, but after they have surveyed such a spread it is not uncommon for them to gain altitude or circle wide around it. Rarely will mature birds either come in low or show signs of actually decoying, and any birds that may decoy are usually juveniles. Consequently when a large number of decoys is used, there should be "holes" within the spread. Not only do these "holes" add realism to the rig, they also become spots where decoying birds are very likely to land. Position your blind within range of these "holes" and you will be in for some sporty shooting.

When a big decoy spread is used for ducks, all of the decoys are usually within gun range. Consequently any duck that flies low over a decoy is in kill range. You have a different situation in goose hunting, especially when snow and blue geese are involved. These birds are lured easiest by great numbers of decoys, and it is not uncommon for hunters to set out spreads containing several hundred decoys, which, when properly spaced, cover a considerable area. Snow and blue goose hunting is bigtime waterfowl hunting in my home state of Texas, and I have frequently gunned for these birds over spreads that contained 500 decoys. This does not mean 500 full-bodied decoys. Rather such rigs are combination spreads of full bodies, silhouettes,

Author's daughter Laura June examines a blue goose that was bagged when it decoyed to a rig of white rags spread in a prairie.

and rags or diapers. Even so when properly spaced such a spread covers a lot of ground, and a hunter spotted dead center in such a spread is likely to discover the decoys on the perimeter are out of effective gun range. Hence if a lone hunter works from such a big spread, he must have "holes" within the rig to pull birds into range.

The style of Texas goose hunting, however, is not to hunt alone. It is more than a one-man job to set out such a big spread. So most of these Texas-size goose spreads are hunted by two or more gunners. They spread themselves across a rig so that wherever a goose flies low over a decoy, it will be within gun range of at least one of the hunters. On several occasions I have hunted 400 to 500 decoy spreads with six companions. One hunt in particular that stands out took place on a near-freezing morning on which visibility was sharply reduced by mist and drizzle. We got our spread set in a plowed field and neither saw nor heard a goose for a half hour. It was one of those mornings when the geese left their roost later than usual. Finally they decided to head for feed, and since we had our spread, bisecting a direct line between roost and feeding area, we had the birds coming straight in.

To make a long story short every man in the party got his limit of snow geese. Seven hunters totaled 35 birds. Not a single bird was taken pass-shooting. Every bird bagged was one that had set its wings and decided to join company with the decoys. The incident points up an important fact about certain species of geese. Snows and blues are very easy to decoy in rough weather when a big spread is used. It seems the dirtier the weather, the more they want to join company on the ground.

A large number of decoys may cause one to suppose the spread cost a lot of money. This would be true if the rig included only full-bodied decoys. Actually the cost of a big spread can be surprisingly low. For example, for snow and blue goose hunting I can field a spread of 500 decoys. This includes two dozen full-bodies, six dozen silhouettes, four dozen diapers and 356 shells made from aluminum sheeting. I accumulated the rig over a number of years so the pains of expense were not big in any given year. Furthermore I only bought a dozen of the full-bodies, two dozen silhouettes and made the rest. The 356 aluminum shells are also made in my spare time. As a result the actual cash outlay for the entire spread was right at $100. Doing it yourself can save a wad of cash, for had I purchased these same items ready-made into goose decoys, the cash outlay would have been in the vicinity of $800.

It is impractical for one man to attempt to use such a large spread. It requires three people to haul my 500-piece rig into a field if the distance is short and the walking easy. If the haul is a long one over boggy terrain, it takes four to pack the load. Furthermore it requires about 20 minutes for three hunters to set out the complete spread.

I generally hunt with one or two companions and find it unnecessary to use the 500-piece spread. We usually set out the two dozen full-bodies, two dozen silhouettes, and about 100 aluminum shells. The only time I bother to use the complete rig is when the hunting party numbers five or six gunners.

Although I have killed countless limits of snow and blue geese over spreads of 30 to 40 decoys, I prefer to use rigs numbering at least 100 decoys. The difference is time, and as one grows older one becomes more acutely aware that time grows less and less. I would rather use the big spread and get my goose limits in a couple of hours than spend the entire day to get the same number of birds over a small rig.

All species of geese don't work to decoys in the same manner. Consider the white-fronted goose, which is also called the speckle-belly. This goose has a strong dislike of lighting with other species of geese. They will work to Canada, snow and blue decoys, but they will swing wide and set a hundred yards or so off to one side of the rig.

Canada geese when working to decoys tend to do a lot of "casing the joint" from low altitude—50 to 100 feet. These birds are extremely cautious and before actually coming in to set, they are likely

Note attitude of these snow geese. Necks are outstretched and feet are tucked well back against their tails. This attitude indicates these birds are not ready to decoy.

to circle wide around the entire field in which the decoys are located. They may do this several times, and the long waits for the birds to move into gun range can indeed be nerve-racking. The Canadas almost always come down behind the spread, therefore the rig should be located some 30 to 40 yards upwind of the hunter's hide. If the spread is split into two rigs side by side, Canadas may work to the open spot between. This opening should be about 30 yards across.

The only time Canada geese lose some of their caution is in a grainfield where spillings are quite obvious. Then they often drop right down into the rig proper. The snows and blues, species that sometimes act downright stupid, are more inclined to drop down into the middle of a spread if there is sufficient open space.

Snow geese are the least particular of all in their approach to decoys. They will often come right in without any circling whatsoever when big spreads are involved. They may do considerable weaving from side to side when they are still well downwind of the spread, but this seems to be an altitude-losing maneuver. When a small decoy spread is used, snows then tend strongly to circle and mill high over the rig, and then when these birds do drop to set, their tendency is to move to the head of the spread.

Snows and blues seem to have one-track minds when they actually start decoying. You can start your shooting and some of the birds may even land in the midst of all the commotion. This is not so with Canada or speckle-belly geese. The sound of the first shot will cause these birds to bolt for the horizon.

In spite of all their caution, I get the impression that geese pay more attention to the watch ganders than to the main part of a rig. Otherwise why is it so easy to pull snows and blues right down into the center of the spread when it often contains nothing more than newspaper sheets, white rags and diapers.

The most difficult aspect of hunting geese over decoys is that of waiting for the birds to get into range. Even when their minds are set to decoying, they can spend an awful lot of time meandering and milling before making their final approach. Many hunters flub the dub during this long wait because of their inability to remain still. They just can't resist the temptation to look or start bringing up their guns. Don't make a move or grab for the gun until the birds have dropped their feet and are just 15 or 20 feet off the ground. You can get away with limited movement when ducks are working in but never with geese.

When geese are moving in formation like this, they are bent on flying a long distance and are not interested in coming down to decoy spreads. The above geese are snows and blues.

When hunting a grain field, place the decoy spread where the spillings are most evident. An excellent way to find the ideal spot is to visit the field a day or two prior to your actual hunting day. Note where the birds are feeding, and then on the day you hunt spread your decoys accordingly. Be sure to get the rig out well before first morning light, for geese leave roosts shortly after sunrise.

It is useless to attempt to decoy geese to rough water where there are breaking waves. Under such conditions the birds will invariably light on land. Except in the case of lush grainfields, ducks will always go to water to light, even if the water is rough. If the water is too rough for them to paddle about on, they will head for the shoreline. The divers will remain on the shoreline, although the puddlers may walk some distance up onto the land if vegetation is sparse enough to permit walking. Sea ducks such as scoters and eiders are at home on rough water. Geese, however, like their water calm.

It is interesting to note how puddler ducks and geese light on land. They touch down first with their feet, but the ducks frequently tumble forward on their breasts in a sort of semi-crash landing. Geese have more poise and balance and rarely lose equilibrium. Any lack of grace on the part of decoying geese is most likely to be exhibited by the juvenile birds. In their haste to lose altitude, they sometimes tumble and flutter like a falling leaf, but they always regain composure a few feet off the ground and settle down majestically.

As with ducks, pay careful attention to the attitude of a goose's feet. As long as the legs are folded back flat against the body and the feet are tucked up under the tail, the bird has not made up its mind to come down. But when the legs are away from the body and the feet are spread to each side of the tail, get ready. This is a decoying goose. Just don't spook it by moving a single muscle.

12

Decoys for Geese

Authentically shaped and realistically painted decoys are absolute musts for some waterfowl species. The Canada goose, the aristocrat of all geese, is such a bird. It will not descend to shoddy decoys. Snow and blue geese on the other hand will work to the craziest of spreads —spreads in which the individual objects used for decoys resemble geese about as much as a submarine looks like an airplane. Really only two things are necessary for a spread to be effective for snows and blues: the spread must be big and it must be white.

A half dozen good decoys spotted on a pond will put a hunter in business when it comes to ducks. A half dozen full-bodied Canada goose decoys will pull in an occasional honker if the hunter happens to be in an area frequented by these big waterfowl. But a half dozen snow goose blocks, even full-bodied models with authentic finishes, will get a fellow only eyestrain and a sore neck. Any snow or blue goose that shows an inclination to work to so small a rig as a half dozen, even a dozen decoys, is (1) a gravely wounded bird that has to set down or die in flight, (2) a stray bird dog-tired from a long flight and badly in need of rest, or (3) a lost juvenile looking for company.

There is no question that full-bodied, realistically painted decoys are far superior to anything else when snow and blue geese are concerned. Two facts usually rule against using spreads composed entirely of such decoys. The spread must be large in order to be seen from a distance, and this means a rig of at least four dozen. Depending upon the brand used, full-bodied goose decoys sell in a price range from $30 to $60 a dozen. The next problem is transportation. Goose decoys are big and they are heavy. There is no sweat if one can drive right up to the blind to unload gear. The trouble is most blinds that

This is a photo of the author's son Carl when he was 12 years old. Note huge size of the snow goose. Goose decoys must be correspondingly large.

can be so reached show so many signs of civilization's wear and tear that birds shun them unless the decoy spread is of such proportions as to hide car tracks and whatnot.

Fortunately for the goose hunter the birds he seeks are more land than water creatures. This means he can effectively use the "shell" type body decoy in place of the full body. "Shell" bodies are bottomless so they can be nested one atop the other for easy carrying. Cross-tree sticks are fitted inside the bodies and then the decoys are staked out in the field. A single hunter can tote four dozen of these decoys—the bodies nested in one tow sack with the heads and necks in a second sack. Prices for these decoys range from $25 to $36 a dozen.

The drawback is these decoys break rather easily. A five or six pound goose blasted out of the sky can smash a "shell" body, and if one does a lot of hunting, this breakage can run into a considerable figure. For example, I lost 21 decoys in this manner alone in a single season. When a person invites one duck hunting, the usual admonition is: "if a duck lands in the spread, don't shoot any of my decoys." You don't shoot geese in the decoys either. You shoot them over the decoys, but you have no control over where the goose will eventually hit the ground.

A third type of commercial goose decoy is called the shadow, also silhouette or popup. It is a two dimension decoy that looks fine from the side, but it is a decoy that "disappears" when birds look down on it from overhead. Prices run from $14 to $20 a dozen. The drawback of these decoys is weight. They pack into compact bundles, but a bundle of four dozen is going to weigh right around 40 pounds, dry weight. Even though they are coated with wax as a protection against the elements, they still manage to absorb some moisture, and this in turn limits their life. If you hunt only three or four times a season, shadow decoys may give you eight or ten years of service, but if you hunt as often as I do, figure on two or three seasons at the most.

Fortunately for the snow and blue goose hunter a fellow can get by at a minimum of expense for decoys since these birds decoy to the craziest of things. The rule of thumb is a "big show of white."

Spread a hundred newspapers or white rags or diapers or even large size paper plates over a field. If this spread is in an area frequented by snow and blue geese, you can expect to get some reasonably good shooting. Early in the season, meaning the first week or ten days, such spreads will pull the birds right to the ground. Geese are supposed to be smart birds, but one gets to wondering about their gray matter when snows and blues land in a spread of papers, rags, etc., and just stand there.

As the season progresses, these "cheapie" spreads become less and less effective. Larger and larger spreads are needed to lure birds, and the bigger the spread the more work there is to haul the stuff out into the field and set in place. Fortunately where snow and blue geese are concerned the situation can be remedied with a compromise. Instead of increasing the paper, rag or diaper spreads from 100 to 200 and then to 300, compromise with a dozen and a half shells complete with necks and heads or two dozen silhouettes.

There are other problems connected with newspaper, rag and diaper rigs. None of these spreads are worth a hoot in the rain. Since newspapers are so easy to obtain, too many hunters never bother to pick them up. They turn yellow, blow all over the field and frighten off birds. Rags and diapers are gathered up for reuse, but oh how they can pick up weight. Not only that, they must be snow white to be effective, and the only way you can keep such a rig white is to run the whole works through the washing machine at the end of each hunt. This can run into a lot of time and work if you hunt 15 or 20 times a season.

A number of materials can be used to make lasting decoys. Materials include poster board, cardboard boxes, sheet plastic and the thin aluminum sheets used on offset printing presses. The poster board, plastic and aluminum sheets are cut out to resemble the outline of a goose when viewed from directly above. Then a V notch is cut in the front end, and the edges left when the notch is removed are overlapped and fastened together with either adhesives or staples. The result is a "shell" body. These bodies nest together, and a hole

These snow geese are decoying on a big concentration of Canada geese. The Canadas, however, are more discriminating and rarely decoy to goose species other than their own.

cut at the apex of each decoy permits a rope or belt to be threaded through for easy carrying. A stack of 50 can be carried comfortably over one's shoulder. All the hunter needs to do is paint the shells flat white both inside and outside, and when this is dry, add black wing slashes on the outside near the tail.

Painting inside and out will seal poster board reasonably well against moisture. There is no problem with either plastic or aluminum soaking up moisture; nevertheless it is important that both sides be painted just in case the wind happens to flip a decoy in the field. The same procedure is used in making decoys from cardboard boxes, only there is no need to cut a V panel out of the front since the configuration of the box naturally forms a tent. A couple of coats of paint inside and out will be needed if cardboard is used, otherwise the material will soak up moisture like a blotter. With reasonable care and unless used in drenching rains, decoys made from poster board or cardboard boxes will last for four or five seasons.

Plastic and aluminum sheet decoys will last indefinitely, although care must be exercised in freezing temperatures. Plastic becomes brittle in cold weather and has a tendency to crack if it glazes over with ice. Aluminum will quickly coat with ice and from wind chill at that. I had an interesting occurrence the first season I used aluminum shells, and it is a story worth repeating.

I carried the aluminum shells nested and then strapped inside a backpack. A total of 70 shells plus the backpack weighed approximately 25 pounds. It fitted nicely on one's shoulders and back, and there was no strain in packing it a mile or so across a field. But it was something else in wet weather when the temperature hovered near the freezing mark. I had my experience on a day when the temperature stood at 34 degrees with a light rain falling and the wind zipping out of the north at 25 miles per hour. The 25 mph wind at 34 degrees brought the wind chill index well below the freezing mark, and with no "body heat" in the aluminum shells the temperature on the surface of the decoys was at what one might call "instant freeze." Anyway the rain drops hitting the decoys did not splatter and run off. Instead they seemed to freeze instantly to the surface. My hunting partner and I killed our limits of geese in less than an hour. Yet in that short time each aluminum shell glazed over solid with ice an eighth of an inch thick. This does not sound like much ice and it is not until the total surface area of each decoy is multiplied by 70. The result turned out to be equivalent to a 20-pound block of ice. So the decoys and the backpack that weighed 25 pounds on the way out into the field almost doubled in weight on the return trip to the car. The load was made more pronounced when the return jaunt included approximately 35 pounds of geese.

When purchased in large lots of 100 sheets or more, poster board will average about 20 cents a sheet, plastic about 35 cents a sheet and aluminum around 18 cents a sheet. Tracing templates should be sized so that two decoys can be made from each sheet since the sheet sizes are approximately 33 by 24 inches. Hence a batch of 100 sheets will yield 200 decoys. Unused aluminum offset printing press sheets are expensive, but newspapers can use a sheet only once. Then papers dispose of the used sheets at whatever prices they can get. These sheets have printing engraved on one side, but this is no problem since it will be covered with paint anyway.

A good sharp knife is needed to cut decoys from cardboard boxes, and the corrugations between the surfaces make the job difficult. Poster board, plastic and aluminum sheeting, which is .009 inches thick, can be cut easily with large scissors.

Flat paints must be used on these decoys. Gloss or semi-gloss paints will shine and reflect light. Personally I prefer latex paints to oil-base paints on two counts. The colors are flatter to begin with, and since decoys get dirty, those finished with latex paints are the easiest to clean.

How well finishes stay on plastic and aluminum shells depends upon the care given them in travel. If they are packed firm and carried in a backpack in such a manner that they won't rub, the finishes won't scratch off. It is worthwhile to pay particular attention to any mars or scratches on the aluminum decoys. There is no sweat if the scratch is not all the way down to the bright aluminum surface. But if it digs that deep, either leave the decoy in the pack or cover the

These geese—snows far left and far right and blues center—are over decoy spread and in gun range.

Overhead shot shows distinguishing markings of snow goose (left) and blue goose (right). Both birds are in easy gun range.

scratch with dirt. Metallic flashes will turn geese and make them put on knots heading in the opposite direction.

A distinct advantage of the shell type decoys, whether made from poster board, aluminum or plastic, is the fact that they are shaped like geese and bear realistic colors. There is no way to shape a rag or diaper to make it look exactly like a goose.

A spread of 100, 300 or 500 decoys does not mean you will cause equal numbers of geese to come down. In my more than 30 years of waterfowl hunting I don't recall more than a handful of times when I had more than a dozen or so geese work into the decoys at the same time. There have been times when I had several hundred geese on the ground in the decoy spread, but these were times when I was not hunting but only observing. Nevertheless the birds did not come in all at the same time but dribbled in over the space of a half hour or so.

It is common for a flight of several hundred birds to vector on a big spread, but rare are the occasions when all the birds come down. Usually a half dozen to a dozen birds will break out of such a flight to work into the decoys. After they get down and all seems well,

FLYING GOOSE

Neck out-stretched

Feet tucked
against body

DECOYING GOOSE

Neck curved

Feet away from body,
webs partially spread

another small group or two may circle back to decoy. The birds that break out of flights are families. Sometimes it will be a single family of the parent birds and a couple of juveniles. At other times several families may descend at the same time.

Generally speaking the goose hunter who keeps tabs on the big flights is just wasting his time. I have seen hundreds of occasions when gunners watched the big flights so intently that they missed ever seeing a small family slip into the decoys from one side. I have seen a lot of hunters embarrassed no end when they stepped out of their blinds to stretch their legs or make a nature call and then have three or four geese sound off loudly and leap out of the decoy rig. This usually happens when the spread contains several hundred decoys.

The easiest geese to decoy are the singles, doubles, and juveniles. These birds are invariably looking for company. If your spread happens to be in their line of flight, and they have not been dusted recently with shot, you can almost bet money they will descend into effective gun range. If the singles and doubles are adults, they may make a reconnoitering circle before descending, but in the case of juveniles they often come in with reckless abandon.

When a family of geese starts to work the decoys, the hunter should take his cue from the lead birds. This bird is always one of the parent birds. The remainder of the birds in the family will key on the leader and act accordingly. Wise hunters know how to use this to their advantage, and when snow and blue geese are involved, they can often cull a full limit from a single family. They down the lead bird, and when the leader goes down, the juveniles in the family often become so confused that they will start decoying on the fallen bird. Even after being shot at, juveniles frequently swing back and try to come down to the leader. The mate of the fallen bird may mill in the area, but it will do its wheeling and calling from a distance well outside of gun range. Only the juveniles are so incautious as to do their milling inside of gun range.

13

Adults and Juveniles

If on a given day some birds readily decoy but others tend to be extremely wary and shy away from your rig, you can pretty well bet there is something wrong with the spread.

Perhaps there is a decoy out there with a line looped over its neck. This can happen when the blocks are set out in the dark. Or maybe a couple of blocks are so close together that they keep bumping. It could also be a matter of too many decoys on the pond. Or perhaps the rig contains too many blocks of one sex and not enough of the other. For example, in this respect spreads predominantly drakes are the most effective early in the season. Toward the latter part of the season a spread should have drakes and hens about equal in number.

It all dovetails in with migration habits. In the case of geese, the entire family—dad, mom and the kids—rustle their down southward at the same time. A few species of ducks follow suit, but most clans don't. Duck family ties are loose at best. Ducklings follow in the shadows of mom's tail feathers but only until they develop their flight feathers. After that they strike out on their own, and for the most part these are the birds that head southward first each fall. In the case of pintails and blue-winged teal, juveniles plus mature drakes head for wintering grounds first. Most of the hens, particularly the mature birds, trail at a later date.

Many hunters jump to the conclusion that birds that swing right into the decoys are birds that have not been subjected to gun fire. In the northern tier of states this could very likely be true, but it is highly unlikely the case in the southern states. These birds most certainly have had charges of shot hurled at them many times in every state from Minnesota southward to Texas.

Then how does one explain the fact that one flight pitches into the decoys with no more than a single circle, while the next bunch circles and wheels time after time and then goes down well out of gun range?

The difference may be in the ages of the birds. Those that drop right in are almost certain to be juveniles. They can be fully feathered, richly colored drakes and still be juveniles, although unless closely examined, a hunter might take them for adult birds. Those birds that circle nervously and then decoy out of range most likely are adults.

Immature birds lacking in experience will stool to shoddy decoys haphazardly tossed out on the water. But with the adults, everything has to be just right.

It is impossible for the layman to distinguish a juvenile from an adult when ducks are flying. But with the bird in hand it is an easy task. Note the tail feathers. If the tip is notched, the bird is a juvenile. The tip of an adult's tail feather is pointed or round. The notching on the immature bird's tail feathers is the result of the downy tip breaking off. This tip will not fill out to become pointed or rounded until the bird is almost a year old. Another clue to age can be found in the markings on breast feathers. Those on the adult female are

The "dirty white" of this snow goose identifies it as a juvenile bird. Juvenile geese are easy to lure to decoys.

V-shaped, while those on the adult drake are U-shaped. These markings are within the feather itself and are not in the outline. On the juvenile bird these markings begin to show indistinctly at the end of the feather and not well back into the feather proper.

With some species of ducks plumage of drakes and hens looks almost alike, and in flight the sexes may be indistinguishable. The black duck is a prime example. Check feathers and bills for sex identification. The drake black duck's bill is yellowish with no markings other than the black nostril and black nail (tip of bill). The hen's bill tends more toward yellowish-orange and is mottled with black markings. The markings on the drake's feathers are U-shaped, while those on the hen are V-shaped. If these markings are lacking or very indistinct, the bird is a juvenile, and then you have to go back to the bill for positive sex identification. The black duck has orange legs, and at one time it was thought that black ducks with red legs were a subspecies. This is not true. Those with red legs are simply very old individuals.

Black ducks are hard to decoy as it is. Anytime you lure in and drop a blackie with red legs, you can rest assured that your decoy spread had a mighty authentic look.

When it comes to geese in a given species, sex plumages are so alike there is really no point in making any distinctions on the decoys. Still with geese it is important to be able to determine an adult from a juvenile, for immature birds are far easier to decoy. This is especially true when young birds have been separated from their parents, and naturally, during a hunting season there are a lot of separations. Young geese separated from their parents seek to join up with other geese of the same species. They won't move right into the flights but will tag along as tail-enders.

Should you have a good looking decoy spread out, an orphaned juvenile that is already tired of flying is very likely to give up its position as tail-end Charlie and come right on down. Meanwhile the group to which it attempted to attach will go winging on, paying not the slightest heed to your decoys.

Juvenile snow or blue geese are easy to distinguish in the air. The immature snow has the white body and black-tipped wings like the adult, but its white feathers will show a lot of gray. Or to put it this way, the adults are the snow-white birds, while the juveniles are those with tattletale gray.

The adult blue goose has a bluish-gray body with vivid white markings on the ends of its primary flight feathers. The neck and head are white. The immature blue is completely slate-gray with white on the lower portion of its belly and up the sides of its rump. Snows and blues fly together, and some naturalists maintain they are one and the same species with the blues simply being a color phase.

The strong parental ties make it possible for a hunter to completely wipe out a small family of geese. Suppose you have five snows
or blues working in toward the decoys. The gaggle includes two
adults and three juveniles. If the adults are bagged first, the juveniles
will continue to mill overhead and often stay within gun range. Should
one of the downed adults be a cripple, the juveniles will decoy on
this bird if the hunter just stays still in his blind.

While juveniles put all their faith in their parents, the parents
in turn are not so trustworthy. Should the hunter knock down a juvenile first, the adults won't hang around and grieve over poor junior's
demise. They will make knots heading for the horizon, probably
telling the remaining juveniles tailing along behind that dead junior
was just a stupid dolt. And if these juveniles survive the season, they
will have occasion to repeat this wisdom to their kids next year.

In spite of the fact that juveniles are so easy to identify, there is
absolutely no need in using decoys finished off to resemble immature
geese. Juveniles just won't decoy to juveniles. They take all their
leads from the adult birds. Therefore if you make your own goose
decoys finish them off to resemble adult birds. Forget all about the
plumage of the immature birds.

14

Downed Birds

One of the surest ways to turn away a decoying flock of ducks is to allow one of their dead brethren to bob on the water with the decoys. If the bird falls within the bulk of the spread, it is likely to be unnoticed by the incoming birds, but if it is floating outside the rig, the birds are almost certain to chandelle for healthier places.

Yet an alarming number of hunters violate the tenet of immediately retrieving downed birds, especially so when shooting over a small pond. They go to great expense, time and work to partake in the wonderful sport of duck hunting, and then fumble it all by being too lazy to retrieve downed birds. They feel it easier to let the wind blow the dead birds to the side of the pond, and then gather them up all at the same time when they quit the hunt.

This is not only a lazy way to hunt but also a most wasteful one.

I have hunted as guest of a few fellows who allowed dead birds to be blown to the bank and left to remain there until the hunt was over. In warm weather they found the flesh of some of the early killed birds had already spoiled. Others with gaping body wounds sopped up mud and again the flesh was tainted. I have even seen varmints sneak out of the marsh vegetation to steal birds that drifted up to the shoreline.

In fact, a few seasons back I put off immediately going after a dead drake pintail because to do so I needed to walk a good quarter mile to get around a very deep slue. The bird drifted to the opposite side of the slue, approximately 100 yards from my blind. I figured on picking it up on the way in because I had to go in that direction anyway in order to return to the hunting camp. Since the weather was quite cold, I knew there would be no spoilage of the meat since I planned to quit in another hour anyway.

In due time I quit, picked up the decoys, and made the long walk around the slue. My duck was still where the wind had blown it against the bank, but it was without head and almost neck-less. There was a great big old nutria dining to its heart's content. This sort of thing isn't supposed to happen, because according to biologists' studies on this huge rodent imported into the United States from South America, the critter is a strict vegetarian. Nevertheless there it was eating my duck. It just proves that there is a nonconformist in every group.

Downed birds should be retrieved immediately, and if the hunter so desires, they can be rigged in a manner to supplement the allure of the decoy spread.

If the sheet of water is very shallow and mud lumps show, arrange the bird neatly atop the lump—facing toward the wind, of course. Tuck the head back under the wing to imitate a sleeping duck, or stick the bill into the mud to mimic a feeder. The same thing can be done on the shoreline if the vegetation is sparse. Should the hunter desire to make the bird look like a swimmer on the same sheet of water, use a forked twig or stick. Shove the twig well into the mud, and then wedge the duck's neck in the fork.

Downed geese can be used to make a duck decoy spread extremely enticing. These birds are big and show up well. They are also very wary and won't decoy unless everything looks just right. Consequently geese added to a duck decoy spread will do much to allay normal suspicion of flying ducks. The dead geese are most effective when rigged on the shoreline or up in the marsh if the vegetation is neither dense nor tall. These birds can be rigged as sleepers, feeders or watch ganders.

It goes without saying that any bird staked out as a decoy should be thoroughly throttled, for it is illegal to hunt over live decoys. Furthermore you don't want the thing suddenly flopping wildly when a flock of ducks is swinging back to the spread. A good neck-wringing will dispatch a bird. Some of the old market hunters used to bite the neck at the base of the head to sever the spinal column. This will kill a bird instantly, but I have never been able to bring myself to doing this trick.

The old market boys used another trick to authenticate their decoys with dead birds. They cut off the wings, folded them back neatly and then glued them to the backs of wooden block decoys. This, of course, was done at home with an eye toward future hunts. A few did it in the field by tying the wings on with string.

A modification of this is still used to some degree today by old baymen hunting over wooden blocks. The modification is to glue only a few of the showy primary wing feathers to the block, rather than use the entire wing.

Some market hunters used to save duck necks and heads. These were dried out and then mounted on long stakes. The stakes were pushed into the ground so the duck heads showed above the marsh vegetation.

15

Water Quality

Water quality has a lot to do with whether or not ducks will decoy to a particular pond. Every waterfowler who has done a lot of hunting has seen marsh ponds that relatively few ducks visit. Yet the same marsh contains other ponds that the ducks regularly use. It's sort of like the village air strip as compared to the metropolitan air base.

Obviously waterfowl have a reason for staying away from certain ponds. It's up to the hunter to find the answer. Sometimes it's easy; other times it's hard. A fellow just throws money away on a lease if he fails to thoroughly examine a pond before signing the lease papers.

For example, there used to be on the upper Texas coast a lake that offered excellent canvasback shooting. The cans were a cinch to be there every season for the lake was one of several containing excellent growths of wild celery, which happens to be caviar to canvasbacks. The territory is also rich in oil, and consequently there are a fair number of producing wells in the area. In this particular case the wells themselves posed no problems either to the hunters or the canvasbacks. Then all of a sudden the cans stopped using the lake, although they continued to fly over the area. The landowner hired a waterfowl biologist to search out the answer.

It didn't take the biologist long to discover a drastic change in the lake's ecology. No longer was the water fresh; it was salty. He found the answer. An oil company had run a barge canal into the nearby land it had leased. This canal, of course, was subject to the rise and fall of the sea tides. On flood tides the water climbed out of its banks and spilled drainage into the lake. The salt water— probably some oil leakage from barges as well—carried into the lake and completely killed out the wild celery stands. The lake now

This is puddler duck as well as diver duck country. Water is shallow enough for the puddlers but still open enough for the divers.

Puddle ducks prefer waters like this. Stand of rushes at left is ideal spot for hunting blind.

has a small levee protecting it and wild celery stands are beginning to return. Only the trouble today is that the canvasback duck population is dangerously low.

Decoys will pull ducks, but they won't lure many if used on ponds that ducks know to be unsuited for their tastes. Remember you only hunt an area once or twice a week, while ducks fly the same area many times a day. They know the locations of the good ponds as well as you know the locations of the light switches in your home.

Check a pond and its shoreline for type of vegetation and abundance of certain types of growths. A pond with stands of widgeon grass, duck potato, smartweed, muskgrass, pondweed, wild rice or wild millet is a cinch to be used as a feeding area. This is the ideal pond for a spread of decoys. Does the pond support animal life? The presence of snails, aquatic insect larvae, minnows, killifish and so forth indicate a likely feeding area. Again, this is the pond on which to spread decoys.

Any pond that fails to support animal life or has shorelines naked of vegetation is one that ducks will avoid. The only time decoys will pull birds to this pond is when new flights move into the territory. They will visit the pond just long enough to discover the water is not to their liking. This is the reason some ponds produce a few days of good hunting and then long slack periods. They are dead ponds until new ducks arrive, and new ducks don't arrive every day of the season. Why waste decoys on such a hit and miss pond? The pond that supports vegetation and animal life complementary to ducks will be a consistent producer of game even with a minimum of decoys.

Some real boners can be pulled when it comes to locating a field for goose decoys. Geese have an affinity to grainfields, but this does not mean they will go to them every time. I have seen geese shun a thousand-acre ricefield and radar in to a forty-acre clover patch. Oh, they love that green stuff and they will visit it every day until the field is stripped bare.

A few years ago I was one of a party of newspapermen invited to a goose hunt near Eagle Lake, Texas, a place that likes to call itself the "Goose Hunting Capital of the World." The afternoon before the hunt we visited the shooting grounds. The owner pointed out blind locations and gave us our choices. Everybody but the landowner questioned my sanity when I picked a pit blind in the middle of a plowed field. The other fellows selected blinds in the rice stubble. The next day I got by far the best shooting.

Old goose hunters can guess the answer. I found out from one of the ranch hands that the field had been plowed the day before we arrived. There were few blades of vegetation showing, but geese find grubbing easy in such a freshly turned field. And the geese were

This is ideal water for ducks. They delight in feeding on this kind of aquatic vegetation. Ducks move to wide open water free of all vegetation when they are nervous and suspicious.

bent on rooting that field I hunted that day. My partner and I had our limits of snow geese and were back in the ranch house enjoying liquid nourishment hours before the rest of the gang returned. The next day I had to surrender that field to a more important member of our party—and he got the banner shooting.

How long is a plowed field good for goose hunting? This all depends upon the weather. If the ground is moist and soft, birds may feed in it daily for as long as a week. Yet if the ground is dry and cakey, the birds are likely to use it for only a day or two.

Puddle ducks, especially pintails and gadwalls, will work to decoys placed in a shallow salt water bay. Just make sure the decoys are spread where the bay bottom is sand or mud. But if the bottom is shell, particularly an oyster reef, then forget it and find a new location, for puddlers don't like shell reefs. Yet a water area with a show of fine gravel is an excellent place for decoys. Ducks like to ingest bits of gravel. It's an aid in grinding up their food. Some of the old market hunters who used to bait ponds for ducks, also spread this fine gravel with the feed to make the place even more attractive. A long deceased uncle who used to hunt for the market told me many

The swimming coot, also known as a mud hen, is not worth hunting, but its presence indicates the water contains aquatic life. If coot shun a water area, so will ducks and geese.

times that a combination of corn, gravel and decoys was unbeatable when it came to attracting game. This combination, of course, is illegal today.

It almost goes without saying that water areas that glisten with an oil film or some other sort of pollution should be avoided. Ducks have pretty good eyes, and they can read the water. Your decoys on a rainbow hued pond will do little to change their minds.

Pick the water on which to spread your decoys as carefully as you would select a wife. The right pick can make for a long and happy life—hunting as well as domestic.

16

Anchors and Lines

Any old piece of string and any old weight will hold a decoy in place. This same "any old piece of string and any old weight" can be the source of both social and financial embarrassment.

Take the time when I was a teenager and was hunting from a point fingering out in a wide, shallow bay. A half hour or so after I spread the rig—actually I just pitched out the blocks haphazardly—a howling norther slammed across the bay. The weights held, but the cotton line, little more than packing string, didn't. The heavy wooden decoys jerked savagely in the wind and rough water, and a lot of lines snapped. I went out with 18 decoys and returned home with 11. The other seven may still be at sea for all I know.

Back in the early 1960s I was a guest at a rather ultra exclusive hunting club. The owner had gone to considerable expense in having duck vegetation planted in the lake, and he had certainly spent a small fortune in constructing three duck blinds. They were elaborate affairs that gave hunters protection from the elements. He had also spotted a hundred decoys at each of the blinds.

"Everything's right for a great shoot tomorrow," he said in greeting us when we arrived early the night before. "The decoys have already been spread. All you fellows have to do is go down to the blinds in the morning."

It was his first year operating a hunting club, and he had failed to take Texas weather into consideration. When Texas northers hit, they hit with no holds barred. And along about two o'clock in the morning we had a dilly of a blow. The wind blew like mad and the camp house shook and shivered on its foundations. It took the front about an hour to pass and then after that the wind subsided to around 10 to 15 knots. When morning came, we were ready to get with the hunting and wasted no time in getting to the blinds. Everything was right except for one thing—the decoys.

That wind had taken its toll. At one blind all the decoys had been blown ashore. Another had its spread blown about a hundred or so yards downwind, and the third had every decoy blown completely to the other side of the lake. In rigging out the blocks the day before, the man, who did all the setting himself, used anchor lines about six feet long and two ounce fishing sinkers for anchors. After a lot of work and lost time we ended up with some fairly respectable hunting for the day, but you can imagine the embarrassment suffered by our host—so much so that it wasn't until a couple years later that he invited us back. Even then he did so in a profusely apologetic way. This time, however, I noted his decoys were anchored securely with eight-ounce mushroom weights.

When it comes to decoy anchors, fishing sinkers will hold if they have sufficient weight—at least four ounces—and the bottom is boggy. Then they will sink down into the mud and hold. On a hard bottom it is far better to go with anchors specifically designed for decoys. They cost much more than fishing sinkers, but in the long run they will save you money and headaches. They come in various shapes and range in weight from four, six, eight or more ounces. Personally I prefer the mushroom type. Six-ounce anchors will do for the general marsh lake, but out on the bays and big lakes where the water can get mighty rough, play it safe with the eight-ounce or bigger anchors.

Now for anchor lines. How about fishing line—say 15- or 20-pound test—for a starter? Okay, but only for pothole shooting where there will be no currents and the water area is so small that it won't get rough. Use this light line on a big lake or bay, and you'll spend more time chasing errant blocks than hunting ducks. Go with strong line, at least 50-pound test.

A cardinal sin in decoy hunting is to use white line or colored line that floats. If the line color clashes too much with the shade of the water, be sure to get the line muddy. This will also make it sink.

It takes more than just weight to hold blocks in place in high wind and rough water. The scope of the anchor line is most important, for if its angle to the bottom is too steep, the block is certain to keep jerking the weight free. A three-foot line is sufficient to hold light plastic decoys in water a foot deep. But if wooden blocks are used, the heavier weight of the decoy is likely to jerk weights free. So with heavy blocks use lines about six feet long.

In deeper water, of course, the lines must be considerably longer —at least three times the depth of the water.

Some open bay shooters rig two to six decoys to a single heavy

Mushroom anchors are superior to other anchor designs in keeping decoys in place in wind and rough water. These are eight-ounce weights.

anchor. The method is to rig one block with a long line to the anchor. The next decoy is tied to the line hole on the bottom rear of the first decoy. Then number three is attached similarly to number two and so forth. The lines between the blocks are about six feet long. This is a good rigging to use unless the water is very rough. Then blocks behind the first decoy are likely to jerk a lot in the waves and often lines between these blocks will be completely exposed. When ducks see lines like this, they shy off. The trailing decoys also have a tendency to make the lead block ride unnaturally in the water. Before going to this rig a fellow should give considerable thought to water conditions.

A glaring fault of this in-line rigging is to get too many blocks lined up in straight lines. This can make a set take a troop marching formation that is completely foreign to the characteristics of wild ducks.

17
Home Made Decoys

With so many authentically shaped and realistically painted decoys on the market today very few waterfowlers ever bother with making their own.

Up until about 50 years ago decoy carving used to be a great art, and many bay and marsh habitues hand-carved and finished every decoy in their spread. They tooled to their individual tastes, and they came up with some excellent tideland sculpturing and art work.

Even though home making of decoys for practical hunting is almost nil now, at some time or other in the career of almost every ardent waterfowler there will arise the desire to carve out a few blocks and heads. They spend many hours at the workbenches, sawing, carving and whittling. More hours are spent with the paint cans. Then they fall so deeply in love with their creations they won't take them into the field for hunting. They can't bear seeing heads or bills broken off, finishes marred or scratched. And so these blocks end up on the mantel or in the den. A ridiculous waste of time? Heck no!

To do the job right, they had to study body and head shapes and colors. In short, they had to research, and whenever a person researches, he gains knowledge. That home-made block may never go into the field, but the fellow who carved it picked up knowledge that will help him when he goes hunting.

I've carved out dozens of decoys, and except for in the mid 1940s and right after I got out of the army, I refused to hunt over them. In those lean years I was too broke to invest in commercial decoys, so for two seasons I had to use a dozen of my creations. They were good, even if I did make them. The fact that ducks were fairly plentiful then may be only coincidental.

This is one of the author's "salvage" decoys. Plastic head was taken from a shot-blasted body and mounted on a body carved from balsa wood. Wood rasp was used to simulate breast feathers. Finish is that of a drake pintail.

Anyway they were so realistic that in the second season of use a very wealthy but casual acquaintance offered to buy them. He offered me a flat one hundred bucks for my dozen pintails and I took it. That buyer enjoyed many good seasons over those blocks.

A complete set of power tools isn't necessary to get into making decoys at home. An electric jigsaw is the most expensive item, but it really isn't needed. Heads can be cut out with a hand jig. It just takes a little longer. Other necessary tools include a hand saw for rough shaping bodies, a drawknife and spoke shave for contouring bodies, a coarse wood rasp for finishing off bodies, and a wood carving knife for detailing heads and bills. Bodies should be smoothed to a final finish with coarse sandpaper. Finer paper is needed for smoothing heads and bills.

Good marine glue is needed for attaching heads to bodies, and, of course, there will be the assorted cans of paints for the final plumage.

Western red cedar and clear white pine are the best woods

These are bluebill and teal decoys the author shaped from cork blocks salvaged from old life jackets.

A beat-up head and body salvaged from the marsh. With a little effort they can be fashioned and reassembled into a good working decoy.

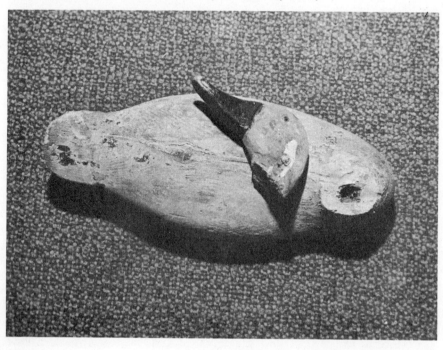

for durable bodies. The same woods are good for heads, although hard balsa is much easier to carve. The balsa, however, is subject to easy breaking, but this is no problem if the mantel is to be the ultimate destination of the decoy. Balsa can also be used for the body unless you plan to hunt over it. Then balsa is a poor choice because it absorbs so much water.

Decoys made of cedar, pine or balsa can be finished into handsome decorative pieces. Cork, another material suitable for bodies, can be fashioned into an excellent working decoy but a poor mantel piece. It doesn't take a nice showy finish that folks like to admire, but it makes an extremely good hen of any species since the finish won't reflect light. It doesn't soak up water like some woods, but it is subject to breakage. It is totally unsuitable for head material.

Even if a fellow never plans to hunt over his home shop decoys, he can learn a lot about the proper shape of decoys and how they should ride on the water. In turn this will enable him to be a wiser purchaser when it comes to getting commercial models. Unfortunately all decoy factories don't put out completely satisfactory products. I have seen commercial decoys with diver bodies and puddler heads and vice versa. These are insults to real ducks.

For example, good puddler decoys should have thick bodies with distinctively upswept tails. If you are making your own, a block 4 x 6 x 15 is the right size for the body starter. Good diver blocks, on the other hand, are less thick but wider and have downswept tails. The starter block for your diver should be 3 x 7 x 14.

The accompanying puddle duck sketch illustrates a good decoy from the side view. With the exception of changes in neck and head shapes, these profiles will stand for any of the following species of ducks: mallard, black duck, gadwall, widgeon and teal. Teal are the smallest of ducks, so the body starter block can measure 3 x 5 x 10.

The diver duck sketch shows profiles for the typical diver decoy. Again the exceptions are found only in the neck and head shapes. The body profiles will stand for canvasback, redhead and bluebill decoys.

Head profiles are important and must match the species of duck they are painted to represent.

Referring back to the puddle duck sketch, note the top is for the mallard, black duck and gadwall. The bottom is that of a pintail. Note the mallard-black duck-gadwall profile tends to an oblong head with neck resting well down on the body. The pintail's head is less bulky and there is a distinct swan-like flare to the neck. Note also that the pintail's tail comes to a point. Teal and widgeon heads are more to the round with a distinct forehead.

The canvasback at the top of the diver sketch has a bill that sweeps back into the head to form a wedge shape. The redhead-

PUDDLE DUCK PROFILES

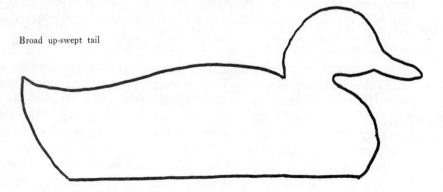

Broad up-swept tail

Mallard, black duck, gadwall, widgeon, teal

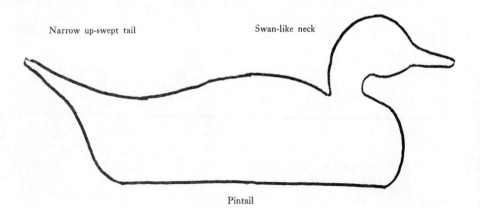

Narrow up-swept tail   Swan-like neck

Pintail

DIVER DUCK PROFILES

Wedge-shape head

Down-swept tail

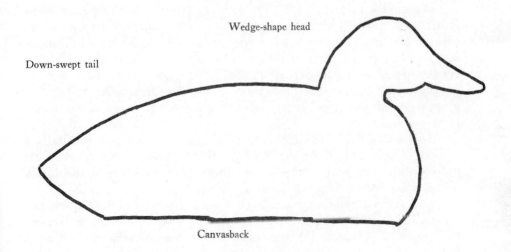

Canvasback

Down-swept tail

Head nestled
low on body

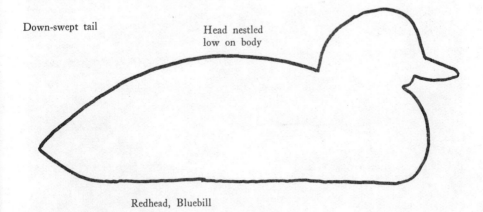

Redhead, Bluebill

bluebill profile at the bottom tends to a more rounded head with a pronounced forehead. Note also this profile indicates a head nestled well down on the body.

Personally I don't like decoys with erect necks, for the impression is that of a nervous bird. If your decoy is being made to be shot over, shorten the neck so the head nestles more on the body. The longer neck is okay if the piece is destined to become a show piece. In this connection show piece decoys should have glass eyes which can be purchased at any taxidermist shop. I have a personal distaste for glass eyes on working blocks, for the glass tends to flash too much in bright light.

Any decoy made for the field will need a keel piece and ballast weight. These should be attached to the bottom of the block with marine glue and brass screws. Skip these accoutrements if the block is intended for decorative purposes only.

The serious minded waterfowler bent on making his entire rig can find excellent plans and patterns in two fine books: *Duck Decoys* by Eugene V. Connett III, published by D. Van Nostrand Company, Inc., in 1953, and *Wild Fowl Decoys* by Joel Barber, published by Garden City Publishing Co., Inc., in 1937.

This homemade snow goose decoy has a body fashioned from .009 thick aluminum sheeting. The head and neck are made from poster board.

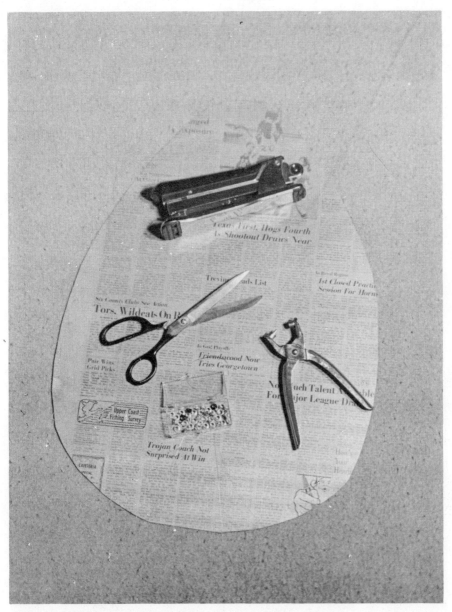

Stapler, scissors, eyelets and eyelet crimper are the tools necessary to make goose decoys from used aluminum sheets used in offset printing.

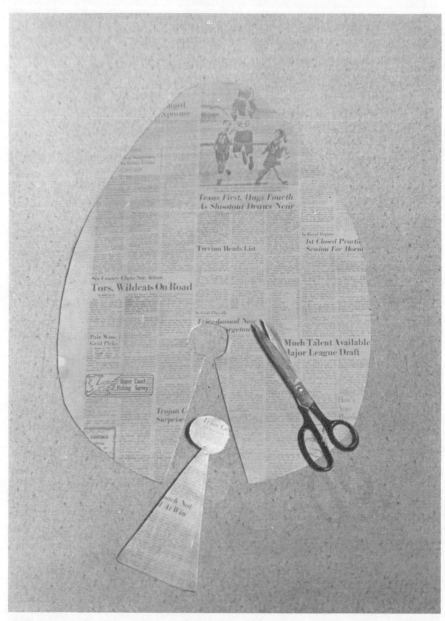

Panel and hole is cut from front end of pear-shaped body. When edges are overlapped, the body takes on tent-like shape.

The edges of the overlap are secured with metal eyelets. Staples can be used but they don't make as secure a fit as the eyelets.

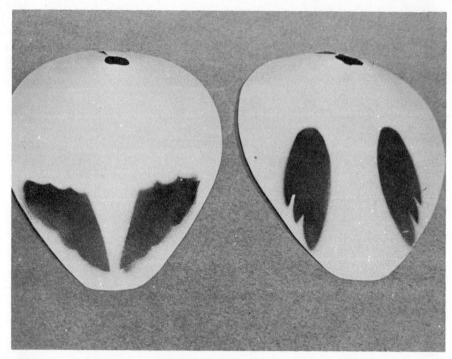

Finished bodies are painted flat white. Templates can be cut from cardboard to allow spraying on of wing slashes. Flat black paint is used for the wing slashes.

Aluminum bodies can be nested for easy carrying. Rope or belt can be run through center hole for carrying.

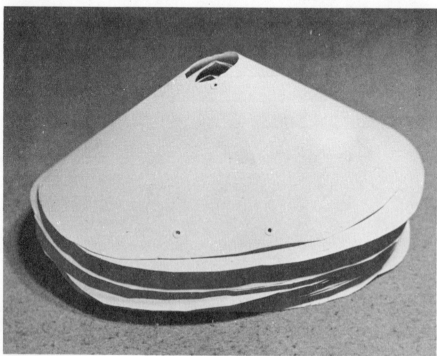

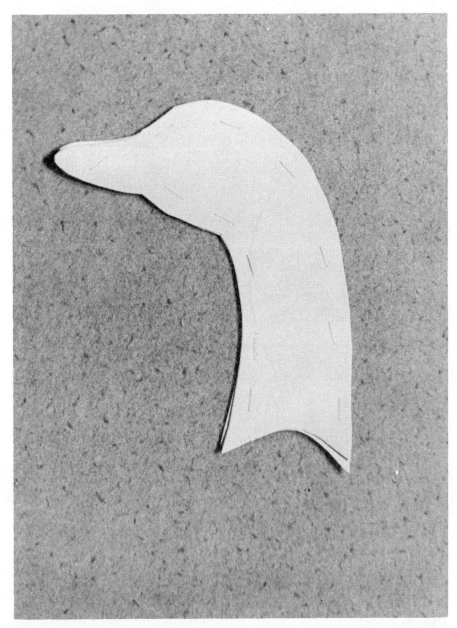

Neck and head to go with aluminum goose decoy is made from posterboard. Two profiles are stapled together for added strength.

Eye and bill details are painted on head. Quarter-inch wood dowel is shoved up through neck. Lower end of dowel is stuck through hole in top of decoy body and shoved into the ground to keep the body in place.

This is a spread of aluminum goose decoys augmented with shadow or silhouette decoys. The aluminum shell bodies are effective even without heads.

18

Painting Decoys

Except for a few very cheap brands, modern decoys are sturdily constructed and will last many seasons. My personal rig includes some with cedar or pine bodies that must be at least 50 years old, molded plastics close to 20 years of age and a dozen inflatable plastics that are still good after 14 seasons.

All of them, however, have been repainted several times. In the case of the wooden blocks, they have been painted perhaps a dozen times. In fact, one started its life as a pintail. Somewhere in its career the head and spike tail were broken off, and I refashioned the tail, carved a new head and turned it into a mallard. Then later, because it rode so low in the water, I carved still another head, reshaped the tail so it took a downward slant and refinished it into a canvasback.

No matter how much loving care a hunter gives his decoys, he will be faced from time to time with a refinishing job. You just can't lug them around in tow sacks, let them stand in all kinds of weather and then expect them to come through unmarred. Sooner or later they will begin to look dingy. When that happens, it's time to haul out the paints and get with it.

Several companies put out decoy paint kits for the more popular species like mallards, pintails, black ducks, canvasbacks, redheads and bluebills. These kits contain all the necessary paints to completely refinish about two dozen decoys. Included in the kits are charts showing how and where the various colors should be employed. Personally I prefer using these kits, mainly because the colors are authentic and flat.

One thing the waterfowler must stay away from in refinishing decoys is paint that dries to a glossy sheen. A decoy finished with such gloss belongs on the mantel or in the den, but not in front of a duck

Left to right are drake pintail inflatable, molded plastic and wooden decoys. Feather details are different on each. Each design is correct, and when mixed in a large rig, the difference adds realism.

blind. Real ducks may be gaily colored, but the colors are not glossy.

If the hunter elects to go with paints other than those found in the kits, then he must be certain to use flat paints. The basic colors are white, gray, black, brown and dark green. Outside house paint is satisfactory, although if a fellow spends a few pennies more and gets marine paint, he will find the finishes stand up longer.

He will have to do a little mixing of colors to come up with the proper shades of blue, purple and bronze-green for wing speculums, and blue, orange, red, yellow or green for bills. Speculums should be flat and minus any gloss. Shine on duck bills won't hurt because the bills of real ducks are usually wet and normally have a shine.

Before a single stroke of refinishing paint is applied, the decoy must be prepared properly. If it is a wooden block of cedar, pine or balsa, sand the body and head with rough sandpaper to remove all scale and dirt. It is not necessary to sand down to bare wood; just make sure all loose paint is removed. A good base is needed for the new paint to adhere to. Take care in sanding the bill. Here use fine sandpaper and avoid any undue scarring. It is important for the bill to have a smooth finish.

In the case of the body and head, however, don't sand the wood too smoothly, since it can tend to give the decoy a glossy finish.

Molded plastic decoys can be prepared by rubbing with steel wool. This will remove dirt and scale from the lands and grooves of the molded-in feathers. Inflatable decoys should be cleaned in warm, soapy water and wiped dry with a bath towel. Use of sandpaper or steel wool on the inflatables can only lead to punctures and leaks.

Completely repainting one decoy at a time is doing it the hard way. You waste as much time cleaning brushes, opening and closing paint cans as you do painting. The work can be speeded up tremendously by going assembly line.

I don't advise applying a base coat of paint to the entire decoy unless it is made of wood. Then a coat of white lead is good to seal the wood against moisture absorption. This is for drakes which normally have quite a bit of white showing. On hen blocks the base color should be the predominant body shade, which in most cases is a shade of brown. When purchasing the paints, you can get the exact shades of brown by getting a can each of burnt umber and burnt sienna.

I finish off bodies first, using the head and neck as a handhold. On

The author carved body feather details on this hen mallard. By not sanding the head smooth, the paint finish takes a feather effect.

All of the feather details on this black duck are painted on. The author added character to the head by carving in the cheek bulge.

The author carved and painted this head for hen bluebill decoy. By not sanding smooth, the finish has a feathery appearance.

some species of ducks the key body shades extend well up the neck and head. These colors could be extended up the neck and heads during the process of body painting, but I have found it rather cumbersome to do when holding a decoy by its bill. It's much easier to complete the neck and head painting after the body is dry. Speculum and bill painting should be done last.

Some gunners believe in going to great feathering details on bodies. This is good if the hunter has only a dozen or so decoys and has artistic talents. If he shoots over a rig of 40, 50 or more blocks, he will find the task of feathering every decoy time consuming. He should, however, put feather details on about a dozen "showboat" decoys. These are the blocks that are spotted around the outside perimeter of the rig, plus those that are strung out at the tail-end of the spread. These "showboats" can be very effective in getting ducks that decoy out of range to swim in for a closer look.

Care must be exercised in painting heads. For example, the head of a drake mallard isn't a solid, single shade of green. It's actually greenish-black. This effect can be obtained by first painting the head a solid green or black. Then while the initial paint is still tacky, stroke on the second color, paying particular attention to having the crown of the head and streak lines in front of and behind each eye more blackish than green.

Pay attention to the drake mallard's white neck color. It does not completely circle the neck. It breaks at the back when the neck joins the body. When the head is completely dry, you can paint on the eye. And right here is where a novice can spoil it all. A mallard's eye is brown—not white, blue or gold.

The same care that goes into a mallard head should be taken in the painting of heads for certain other species. Make the white streak up the pintail's neck, the white half-moon on the front of the blue-winged teal's face and the green comet around the green-winged teal's eye as realistic as possible. These are details that can count when the birds are skitterish.

If you doubt the importance of details, note how crooked hose seams detract from the underpinning of the well-proportioned office secretary.

Equal care should be shown in painting bills. Some years back a decoy manufacturer sent me a half dozen mallards he was introducing to the market. The decoys were authentically shaped, rode the water well and were realistically painted—except for one detail. The drakes as well as the hens all had orange bills. This is okay for hens, but all wrong for drakes. The bill of the drake mallard is yellowish-green. I look at it this way. If ducks were color blind, none would be so gaily colored. The coloring certainly doesn't blend in as any camouflage.

These two photos illustrate what the hunter faces if he elects to paint individual feathers on his decoys.

With this in mind I insist on my decoys having bill colors to match the species. What is more, all bills are not solid colors. The bills on almost all hens are mottled. In the case of drakes, the waterfowler should paint on the nostrils and nails (tips of bills).

Some decoy makers overdo this bit about wing speculums and make them outlandishly large. The speculum of a real duck is rather large

and easy to see—when the bird is flying. But on the water it's another matter. A duck nervous and about ready to take flight will arch its body in such a manner that the speculum becomes clearly visible. That same duck at rest and at peace with the world will nestle down its wings in such a way that the speculum is tucked in and sometimes almost completely hidden. What is the purpose in finishing off your decoy so it gives the impression of being a scared duck?

If the waterfowler insists on detailed coloring on the body, he should spend his time on the back and tail. This is the part of a decoy a flying duck sees in detail.

I guess because it is more fun painting the colorful drakes than the drab hens that a lot of hunters in the course of refinishing decoys change the sex of the block. Decoys are usually sold in sets of a dozen to a set, and each set usually contains eight drakes and four hens. Maintain this ratio. Don't make the mistake of turning every decoy into a drake. If the season is open in the early fall—and it is in some parts of the country—flocks will contain far more males than females. And usually these males group away from the females.

All this changes in late December and early January—particularly in the southern United States. The drakes will begin to mingle with the hens. If the weather is unseasonably warm, the observant waterfowler will even note some birds—especially mallards and black ducks —beginning to pair off. Consequently the late season rig must contain some "showboat" hens.

If you have trouble blending colors to get the proper shades, major paint stores can provide them if you specify the shades by name.

This is one of the author's drake baldpate decoys. Minute details are unnecessary but key feathers and colors should be painted on boldly so that the drakes will stand out in the spread.

Decoys of several species all add realism to a spread. Author's homemade decoys from front to back include drake black duck, drake baldpate and hen mallard.

Most distinctive features on this wild mallard drake are its green-black head, white neck collar, dark breast and black rump with white-tipped feathers.

This mallard hen is one of the author's breeders. Left wing has been clipped to keep bird grounded. This degree of feather detail is not necessary on all decoys.

For example, one of the major body colors on the mallard drake and mallard hen is brown. But just any old brown won't get the job done to perfection. The proper shades to seek are burnt umber and burnt sienna. Depending upon the number of species you desire to represent other major shades needed include: taupe (dark gray), yellow ochre (yellow-brown), olive (green-yellow), buff (cream-yellow), rust (red-brown), flat white, and flat black.

By species the following colors are recommended:

MALLARD DRAKE

BODY: burnt sienna, gray, white, black.
HEAD AND NECK: green, black, white.
BILL: olive, black.
SPECULUM: purple, white, black.
EYE: brown.

MALLARD HEN

BODY: burnt sienna, burnt umber, ochre, white.
HEAD AND NECK: burnt sienna, burnt umber, ochre.
BILL: orange, black.
SPECULUM: purple, white, black.
EYE: brown.

BLACK DUCK

BODY: burnt umber, black.
HEAD AND NECK: ochre, burnt umber.
BILL: (drake) olive, black; (hen) orange, black.
SPECULUM: purple, black, white.
EYE: brown.

PINTAIL DRAKE

BODY: taupe, white, black, ochre, buff.
HEAD AND NECK: burnt umber, white.
BILL: blue, black.
SPECULUM: green, white, black.
EYE: brown.

PINTAIL HEN

BODY: burnt sienna, burnt umber, white, black.

HEAD AND NECK: burnt sienna, burnt umber.
BILL: blue, black.
SPECULUM: green, white, black.
EYE: brown.

GREEN-WINGED TEAL DRAKE

BODY: taupe, burnt umber, black, white, buff.
HEAD AND NECK: rust, green, black.
BILL: blue, black.
SPECULUM: green, black, white.
EYE: brown.

GREEN-WINGED TEAL HEN

BODY: burnt sienna, white, black, burnt umber.
HEAD AND NECK: burnt sienna, burnt umber.
BILL: black.
SPECULUM: green, black, white.
EYE: brown.

BLUE-WINGED TEAL DRAKE

BODY: taupe, black, white, blue.
HEAD AND NECK: black, white, blue.
BILL: blue, black.
SPECULUM: blue, white.
EYE: brown.

BLUE-WINGED TEAL HEN

BODY: burnt sienna, burnt umber, blue, black, white.
HEAD AND NECK: burnt sienna, burnt umber.
BILL: blue, black.
SPECULUM: blue, white.
EYE: brown.

WIDGEON DRAKE

BODY: burnt umber, white, black, tan.
HEAD AND NECK: yellow ochre, white, green, black.
BILL: blue, black.
SPECULUM: green, black.
EYE: brown.

WIDGEON HEN

BODY: burnt sienna, burnt umber, black, white.
HEAD AND NECK: yellow ochre, white, black.
BILL: blue, black.
SPECULUM: green, black.
EYE: brown.

CANVASBACK DRAKE

BODY: black, white.
HEAD AND NECK: burnt umber, black, white.
BILL: black.
SPECULUM: none.
EYE: reddish.

CANVASBACK HEN

BODY: burnt umber, taupe, white.
HEAD AND NECK: burnt umber, ochre, white.
BILL: black.
SPECULUM: none.
EYE: reddish.

BLUEBILL DRAKE

BODY: taupe, black, white.
HEAD AND NECK: black, green.
BILL: blue, black.
SPECULUM: none.
EYE: yellow.

BLUEBILL HEN

BODY: burnt umber, white.
HEAD AND NECK: burnt umber, white.
BILL: blue, black.
SPECULUM: none.
EYE: yellow.

REDHEAD DRAKE

BODY: taupe, black, white.
HEAD AND NECK: black, dull red.
BILL: blue, black, white.
SPECULUM: none.
EYE: yellow.

REDHEAD HEN

BODY: burnt umber, burnt sienna.
HEAD AND NECK: burnt umber, white.
BILL: blue, black, white.
SPECULUM: none.
EYE: yellow.

CANADA GOOSE (sexes alike)

BODY: burnt umber, black, white.
HEAD AND NECK: black, white.
BILL: black.
SPECULUM: none.
EYE: black.

SNOW GOOSE (sexes alike)

BODY: white, black.
HEAD AND NECK: white.
BILL: reddish-pink, black.
SPECULUM: none.
EYE: black.

BLUE GOOSE (sexes alike)

BODY: taupe, black, white.
HEAD AND NECK: white.
BILL: reddish-pink, black.
SPECULUM: none.
EYE: black.

19

Bayman Style

Decoy painting. What will it be—à l'artiste or à la bayman?

You may go artistic on a few, carefully blending the shades on heads and necks to indicate shadows and tediously feathering the individual back, wing and tail feathers. Beautiful, beautiful. So beautiful, in fact, that you refuse to hunt over it for fear of scuffing and marring the finish. So your artistic creation ends up in the den—and the wife gripes incessantly that it is only a dust collector.

But in this book we are not concerned with masterpieces of painting that fellow hunters can admire from arm's length. Our job is to turn out work decoys and paint them for the field.

And duck that gets within arm's length of any of my decoys is going to have its memory and appreciation of details abbreviated by a charge of shot. If the duck is lucky, I'll miss, my gun will jam, or I'll be asleep in the blind. Ducks see decoys from a distance. They move in for a closer look. If you shoot them passing over the spread, they will be 20 or 30 feet from the decoys and traveling at a fast clip. They will be moving too fast to eyeball individual feather details.

So for the purpose of hunting I believe in painting my decoys à la bayman. In this method the proper colors are used but minute individual details are skipped. Instead of painting in all the wing and tail feathers, a few are rather boldly indicated with everything else being solid colors. I can do two dozen blocks bayman style in the same time that would be needed to finish off one in true artistic fashion. I don't want to spend an entire month painting decoys.

The following sketches are my personal schemes. The reader will note that except for the hens represented, there are only a few back feathers indicated on the drakes. This bayman style of painting may be out of character as far as a single decoy is concerned. But we don't hunt with just a single decoy; we use them in groups. Hence the overall appearance is realistic.

Repainting decoys offers one the advantage of getting away from stereotyped uniformity. Feathers can be boldly stroked in on one decoy, and then only faintly indicated on another. The result is a spread with lifelike qualities.

And this is the name of the game.

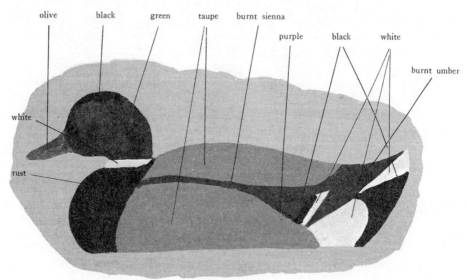

olive   black   green   taupe   burnt sienna   purple   black   white   burnt umber

white

rust

Mallard Drake

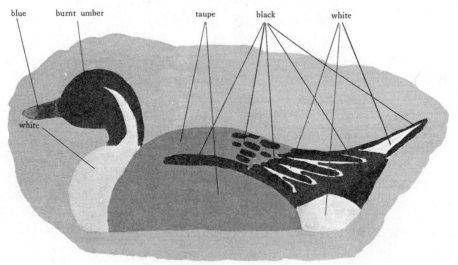

blue   burnt umber   taupe   black   white

white

Pintail Drake

orange

burnt sienna
(feathers burnt umber)

burnt umber
(feathers burnt sienna)

purple

black

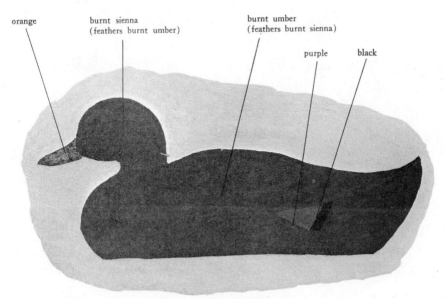

Black Duck

orange

burnt umber

ochre

burnt sienna (feathers burnt umber)

purple

black

white

ochre

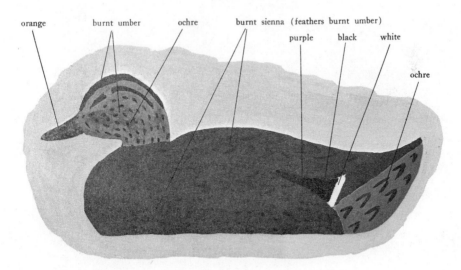

Mallard Hen

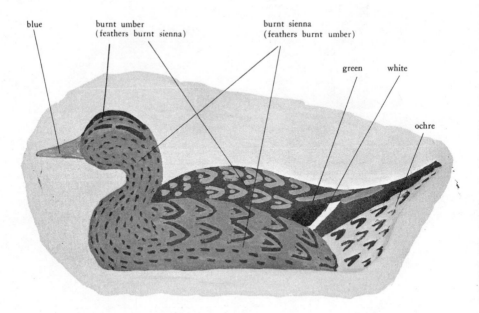

blue

burnt umber
(feathers burnt sienna)

burnt sienna
(feathers burnt umber)

green   white

ochre

Pintail Hen

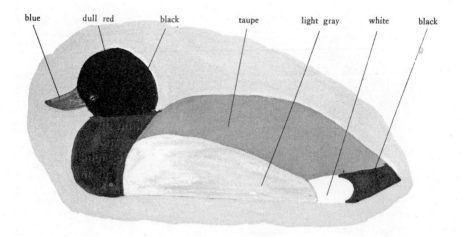

blue   dull red   black   taupe   light gray   white   black

Redhead Drake

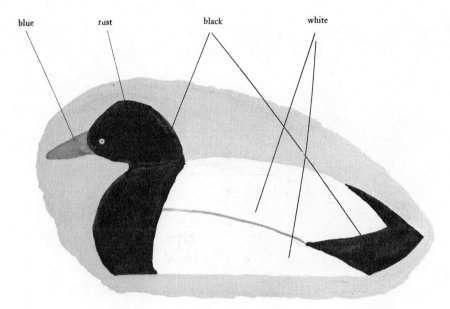

blue   rust   black   white

Canvasback Drake

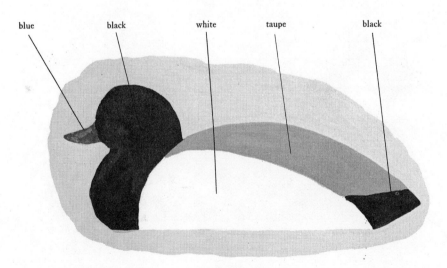

blue   black   white   taupe   black

Bluebill Drake

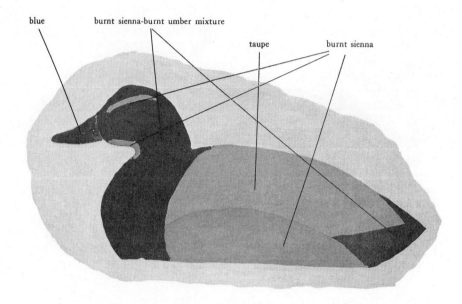

Canvasback Hen

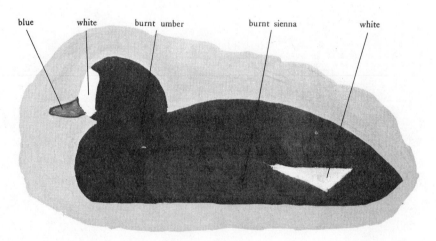

Bluebill Hen

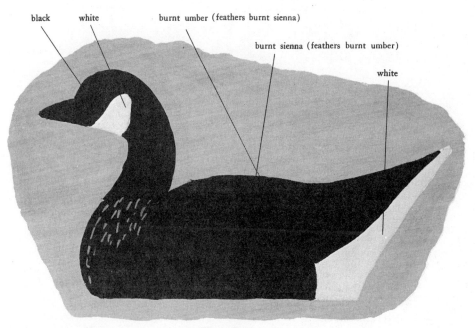

black   white   burnt umber (feathers burnt sienna)

burnt sienna (feathers burnt umber)

white

Canada Goose

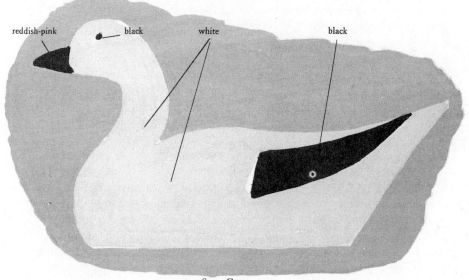

reddish-pink   black   white   black

Snow Goose

20

Silhouettes and Shadows

Without question full-bodied decoys, whether they are for ducks or for geese, are vastly superior to silhouettes, which are sometimes referred to as "shadow" or "pop-up" decoys. The full-bodied decoy with its three dimensions has numerous advantages. It can be seen from greater distances, it can be seen and readily identified from all angles, and above all it is more lifelike. This lifelike bit can mean everything to the hunter when the birds are already spooky.

There are, however, times when the silhouette decoys are a must, and if a hunter knows how to spread them, he can get in some mighty good action. Financial difficulties and portage can force the use of these shadows. For example, last season I hunted snow geese with a fellow who put out four dozen full-bodied decoys. The decoys were made in half shells so that one body fitted snugly in the next for easy portage. The heads were carried separate, and needed only to be popped onto the bodies when the rig was spread. The four dozen could be carried easily in two army barracks bags. The bundles were a little awkward as far as size was concerned but not at all heavy.

There was just one trouble: in the area in which we hunted, the geese moved in huge concentrations. A spread of four dozen decoys was small. A fellow a quarter mile away with a spread two to three times bigger was almost certain to get all the action. Full-bodied goose decoys, however, are expensive. Those we shot over carried a $49.95 per dozen price tag. When one considers the sales tax, the decoys ran well in excess of $50 a dozen. When it comes to hunting geese with a rig composed 100 percent of full-bodied decoys, the sport can become quite expensive.

In order to beef up our rig we supplemented the 48 full-bodied stools with six dozen silhouettes. Actually these were more than just silhouettes. They were made of cardboard, painted to resemble snow

These are cardboard Canada goose profile decoys, also called shadow or silhouette decoys, spread with white rags for snow geese in rice stubble. Snow and blue geese will work to a spread like this, but Canada geese will not unless the Canada decoys are spread off separate to one side.

The body of this Canada goose profile "pops-up" into three dimensions when metal spreader bar is rigged inside the body.

The spreader bar is part of metal spike on which this Canada goose "pop-up" decoy stands. Decoys of this type can only be used on land.

Note how profile decoys compare with full-body decoys when viewed from above. Profiles can be made more effective if slanted so that they will cast a shadow on the ground.

geese and Canada geese, and treated with wax as a protection against moisture. When the bottoms of the bodies were spread out and held open with a metal spread bar, the decoys assumed a tent-like structure. When not in use the metal spreaders and heads folded neatly into the bodies of the decoys. The six dozen were carried in a newspaper carrier's bag. These silhouette decoys cost $14.95 a dozen.

When spreading a mixed rig of full-bodied and shadow decoys, the hunter must take care to space them alternately so that all the shadows are not off to one side. The hunter must always keep in mind the goose eye view. The birds in preparing to decoy will work into the wind and in from behind the rig. Full-bodied decoys will stand out in lifelike detail. The shadows, even the pop-ups that form a sort of tent, can become invisible or misshapen, depending upon the angle from which the approaching birds see them.

If all the full-bodied decoys are in one place and the silhouettes off to another side, the sudden disappearance of half a rig on the ground can cause birds to shy off.

There is a trick the hunter can use to partially eliminate this

Side view of profile and full-body decoys. Note how much more lifelike the full-body decoys appear. They can make the difference between a waterhaul and a good hunt when the weather is clear.

Many types of full-body goose decoys can be disassembled for easy carrying and storage. The type above shows the bodies nested on each other. The heads are made in various attitudes. The wooden cross sticks are for making the decoys stand high enough to be seen from a distance.

Note how cross sticks are fitted in the body. These stakes are important in strong wind to keep the decoys from upsetting.

Stand spike, spreader bar and head fold into the body of this "pop-up" decoy to make for easy storage and carrying.

A major advantage of the full-body goose decoy over the silhouette is that more realistic head and neck attitudes are available. A goose rig in which all the decoys have necks stretched and heads upright indicates suspicious birds. On full-body decoy in photo the neck is bent and the head is down in natural feeding position.

vanishing act. Although the decoys must always be faced toward the wind, the gunner can quarter them at an angle of about 30 degrees off true dead-into-the-wind. Although they may appear misshapen to birds approaching directly into the wind, they at least will not completely vanish.

The hunter should always angle the silhouettes into the direction in which he is hidden. When geese take off, they do so into the wind, but immediately thereafter they tend strongly to turn away from the point of danger or anything that may appear suspicious on the ground. Decoying geese tend to work off toward the side in which the decoys are angled. This means the birds will work in close to the hunter.

Shadow decoys stand on either wood or metal rods stuck into the ground. Another trick to prevent the decoy vanishing act is to stand the decoys at an angle to the ground. Instead of being perpendicular to the ground, lean them over a bit. But lean them all over to the same side. Birds overhead will look down on misshapen decoys, but at least they won't vanish completely from sight.

Actually it is incorrect to call these decoys true silhouettes, for in addition to the side profile of the bird, each decoy is finished off in true markings and colors. In the case of some brands, the finishes are actually photographs that have been reproduced to life size on the cardboard. I rather suspect these two dimension decoys got to be called "shadows" because of the shadows they threw upon the ground when the sun was off to one side. When this happens, the decoys don't vanish when birds are directly overhead because of the shadows. This, of course, works only on a day with bright sunshine. The typical waterfowl hunting day, however, is one with a heavy, dirty overcast, and on such a day there just is not enough direct light for any appreciable shadows. The silhouettes make fine shadows when the light is sufficient and there is snow on the ground.

Commercial silhouettes are made of metal, plywood, composition board and cardboard. Those made from metal or plywood will, of course, last the longest and stand the most abuse. They are also more costly and heavier than the cardboard shadows.

Cardboard decoys will last many seasons if given reasonable care. Most come with the outsides coated over with wax to protect against moisture. The hunter can give the decoys extra protection by melting some wax and painting it over the inside of the decoy if it is the pop-up type that forms into a tent.

21
Acquiring Decoys

Acquiring a rig of decoys via carvings may be interesting, but it is very time consuming. You can't go to the work bench and finish out a dozen in a single afternoon. If they are to be made properly, it requires many long hours. So the easiest way to get a rig is simply to go out and purchase accordingly.

You can buy cheapies for around $10 a dozen. Or you can get exact replicas that may sell for something like $75 a dozen. Adequate and sturdy decoys that will give years of service can be obtained in the $20 to $25 per dozen range. Those $10 sets, usually made of pressed fiber, are okay for occasional hunting, but they won't stand up if a fellow guns 15 to 20 times a season.

The initial price of good molded plastic models often causes some beginners to scrounge around for the old wooden blocks.

"Oh, I can probably pick up a few dozen for twenty bucks," a friend once remarked to me. "A couple more bucks for paint and I'm all set."

The friend made this remark three years before I started this book. He now has two wooden blocks dressed up for his den, but he has none to hunt over.

He made several startling discoveries in his quest for old wooden blocks. His first discovery was that plastic in some form has completely taken over the decoy business. Then he discovered that garages and attics with old blocks are rare. The biggest shocker came when he learned that decoys that sold for $10 a dozen many decades ago did not depreciate. The fact that they are scarce has skyrocketed their value, not as hunting pieces but as collector's items. Some of those old blocks that used to sell for 50 cents to a dollar each now

Wooden decoys such as this are still easy to find. Rough finish of wood makes for effective featherlike appearance. Advantage of wooden decoy is the ability to stand up under rough treatment.

carry tremendously inflated price tags. If the block carries its original finish and some identifying marks as to its maker, it could be an item a decoy collector will pay for handsomely.

Early decoys, even those produced in pioneering factories, were often crude and misshapen. Yet they were effective because they were used in huge rigs and ducks were extremely plentiful. Today ducks are far less populous, consequently decoys now used must represent the birds they are intended to be far more realistically.

It is a fact that uniformity of pose is very rare in any group of birds assembled on land or water. All birds strike a similar pose when they are nervous and alarmed. Then all necks are straight up, heads held high and bodies tensed for a quick, fast getaway. In this respect early decoys had a distinct advantage over today's mass-produced versions. They came in various shapes and sizes. Head poses were varied and often exaggerated. A single decoy may have looked out of proportion to the bird it was supposed to represent, but when used in conjunction with other decoys, the resulting spread was most life-like. There is no doubt that the old market hunters had the best rigs of them all.

Feather details can be made to stand out realistically in molded plastic decoys. These are Italian made green-winged teal. Drake is in the top photo; hen in the lower photo.

These two photos represent a duck's eye view of the same green-winged teal.
Drake is in the top photo; hen in lower photo. Setting special teal seasons in the
1960s led to increased use of decoys representing these game little ducks.

To match the effectiveness of the market hunter's spread today's waterfowler in assembling his rig must blend it to achieve true realism. If he doesn't, he may end up with a rig regimented and tin-soldierish in appearance.

Modern duck decoys are marketed in the following species (drakes and hens): mallard, black duck, pintail, teal, widgeon, canvasback, redhead and bluebill. A complete set, which is generally considered a dozen, isn't necessary in each of the species. Mallard, black duck, and pintail blocks are the main puddler decoys, while canvasbacks and bluebills are the key diver stools. The other species are not necessary unless the waterfowler guns in areas where these ducks are predominant, although in all fairness to the decoy manufacturers, and to the hunters' welfare as well, a few teal or widgeon blocks supplementing a basic mallard-black-duck-pintail rig tends strongly toward realism. I have found this to be especially true for calm water and no wind conditions. This is when the puddle ducks are the wariest about working to the decoys.

All mallards, pintails, bluebills and so forth don't look exactly alike. A rig in which every decoy is a carbon copy in size and coloration can look—to a flying duck—as phony as a three dollar bill. With real ducks, sizes and color shades vary. One mallard drake may have a head tending toward a true green, while on another the head may appear more green-black. The waterfowler will find a wide variance on feather details on drake pintail decoys. One manufacturer may have the distinctive black and white tertiary feathers flaring out; another may have them running straight back. Both patterns are correct. They just represent the duck with its wings folded in different attitudes. The pintail with the tertiary feathers pointing straight back is a peaceful and restful one. This is a good impression to convey to flying birds. The pintail decoy with feathers appearing to flare out is remarkably similar to a real pintail in courtship display.

To obtain this mixture in decoys the waterfowler may have to purchase several different brands of decoys. It is worth the trouble to gain the added realism.

Decoy manufacturers patent their models, which means no other company can produce identical designs. Hence we find noticeable differences in shape, size and color schemes from brand to brand. I can field a spread of 40 mallard decoys representing five different manufacturers. Some are inferior in shape and color, but when all the blocks are spread into a rig, the result is excellent realism. In fact, the spread is so realistic it has been raked several times by sneak hunters. If there is anything good to be said about sneak shooters, it's that they usually can't judge range worth a hoot. They rake the decoys from such long range that the shot just bounces off with no damage done. Once, however, I had these creatures trespass in close enough to blast gaping holes in molded plastic decoys and knock the heads off wooden blocks. And they didn't even have the guts to apologize. They just ran. Had they remained, I still would have been angry, but considerably mellower since their very transgression complimented me on putting out a realistic rig. If the blocks fooled other hunters into thinking they were real, they certainly should do likewise with flying birds. And this happens to be the name of the game.

Some models come with heads and bodies molded as single units. Others have heads and bodies made separately; consequently heads can be removed for easy portage or they can be adjusted on bodies at various attitudes. Just make sure when assembling to match heads to proper species and to proper sexes. This may sound like childish advice since it is so elementary. But it's not quite that simple when setting out blocks in the dark and with life made additionally miserable by cold, wind, or rain—or all three combined.

Just a few seasons back I made this boner, and didn't discover it until a half dozen flights of ducks that wanted to decoy suddenly flared off while still out of range. Then I happened to notice that I had mounted a drake mallard head on a drake pintail body. To

Molded plastic decoys are usually made in shells, bottom and top or two sides. The more expensive models have the join lines finished off smooth unlike the ridged join lines on decoy shown.

magnify the error I had set this monstrosity out as one of the "show-boat" blocks near the tail-end of the spread. And this is the part of the rig the ducks pass over first when working in to decoy. After I went out and made the change, the hunting pattern changed and inside of a half hour my companion and I had the limit of eight birds.

I could have gotten by had I mismatched hen heads and bodies, since the hens of the various species are so similar in color. It's a horse of a different color when it comes to the distinctively marked drakes. To repeat, a fellow can make some stupid mistakes when he attempts to act with haste in the dark. And this isn't limited to just duck hunting.

Mallards and pintails occasionally cross breed. The results are hybrids that show some rather outlandish color patterns. I've seen hybrids on hunting grounds, and I've killed two. In the case of both kills the birds were loners that came into the decoys as singles. Observing unmolested bunches of ducks on the water and bunches in which a hybrid appeared, I noted in most cases true drakes of the pure strain species had strong tendencies to pick on the hybrid birds. I've seen hybrids chased away from the flock, and I find it difficult to decide its social standing with the flock. I just know I don't want any hybrid decoys in my rig.

The most popular duck species for which decoys are made to resemble are mentioned earlier in this chapter. In addition there are a few small manufacturers who specialize in other species. These are for ducks that may be abundant in small regions of North America. For example, you can find old squaw decoys available along the upper New England Coast, and scoter blocks around the Great Lakes and upper New England seaboard.

The New Englander who moves to Texas and hauls along his scoter decoy rig is going to be very unhappy with his hunting. Scoters are so rare in the Lone Star State that when one is killed, the story complete with pictures gets feature play in the newspapers. By the same token the Californian who lays in a supply of black duck decoys is spinning his wheels. Black ducks are very rarely found west of the Mississippi River. Those that are will be in zoos or aviary gardens, not in the wild. Then there's the case of the common goldeneye or whistler. Decoys representing this species are common in the eastern states, around the Great Lakes and up the Atlantic seaboard north of Florida, but you won't find this decoy used in the Southwest.

Consider the Canada goose and its subspecies. These birds are found in some number in almost all states. The American brant and black brant, which are true salt-water geese, occur in very restricted areas. The black brant is found along the Pacific Coast, while the American Brant winters along the middle section of the Atlantic Coast.

Snow geese are extremely populous, yet their wintering range is

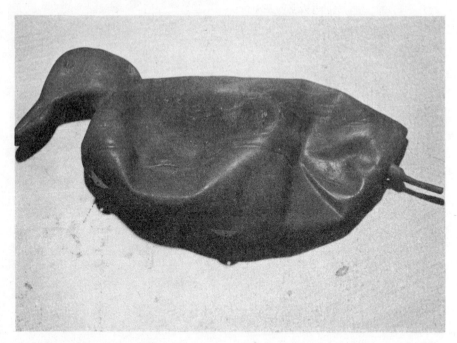

A dozen rubber decoys like this can be rolled up and carried in a hunting coat pocket. These rubber inflatables work well on small ponds but tend to bounce and flop too much on rough water.

limited to the Pacific Coast, Atlantic Coast and Gulf Coast, including Texas, Louisiana and Mississippi. The range of the blue goose is even more restricted. It is limited almost exclusively to the Louisiana and upper Texas coasts.

Therefore in assembling a decoy rig, the waterfowler should fit it to the section of the continent in which he lives.

The key to duck species most frequently encountered in various parts of the country can be found on the maps that accompany each individual bird species in *Birds of North America* by Chandler S. Robbins, Bertel Bruun, and Herbert S. Zim and published by Golden Press in New York in 1966. The book is basically a field guide for bird watching, yet its handy size (small enough to slip into a hunting coat pocket) and numerous color sketches of duck species in various flying attitudes make it an invaluable aid to the hunter.

In antique shops, stacked in the corner under a layer of dust in the attic, and in sacks in dark nooks of old barns, there still exist wooden decoys of yesteryear.

Occasionally some return to the light of day but seldom as tools for the hunt. These old blocks—chipped, weather-beaten and in various states of repair—may never again undulate on the water to lure mallards, pintails, canvasbacks and such to their doom. If they are used in the field, it will be by persons not knowing better. And then when they discover what they have been doing, they may find themselves bordering on cardiac arrest.

Today's waterfowler who happens upon a sack of old wooden blocks should check them out carefully. Go over each individual block. Most are likely to be run-of-the-mill decoys turned out since the turn of the century. Some of these makes may be numerous enough so that individual blocks have little value to a collector. They can be dressed up and hunted over again.

But it's a different story with those weather-beaten blocks that look like they are a hundred years old. They may be that old and worth a small fortune to a collector. Clean off the dirt and nothing else. Then start checking them out for value.

Complete details on old decoys and decoy collections can be found in two excellent books. These include *Wild Fowl Decoys* by Joel Barber, published in 1937 by Garden City Publishing Co., Inc., and *American Bird Decoys* by William J. Mackey, published by E. P. Dutton & Co., Inc., in 1965.

22

Repair and Storage

Ray Bowen, with whom I often hunt, is one of the better known waterfowlers in Texas. I made my first hunting trip with Ray back in the fall of 1946. We had climbed back into the blind after setting out a spread of 60 decoys off a point fingering out into Galveston West Bay, when he casually remarked: "Be careful not to shoot any of my decoys."

I'm sure such a remark would offend some hunters. They would consider it an insult to their intelligence. Nevertheless I feel it is an appropriate remark to make to a first time hunting companion. Good hunters don't shoot decoys on purpose, but good hunters have been known to inadvertently pepper the blocks. They shoot at a bird that passes very low over the rig and fringe shot rattles the decoys. Or they bear down on a cripple on the water and fail to realize a decoy or two a few yards beyond the bird is in the direct cone of shot.

In one respect the old wooden blocks have a tremendous advantage over today's modern plastics. They can absorb a lot of stray pellets with no serious damage. At the worst a head or bill might be knocked off, but regardless of how hard hit a wooden block may be, it won't sink.

Most of the modern plastic decoys will turn normal-size waterfowl shot—sizes 5, 6, and 7½—at 40 yards. Larger pellets—BB, 2, and 4—are almost certain to penetrate. And it seems like all the penetrations are invariably around the waterline. This means a sinking decoy. What are you going to do about it? Let it sink and forget it?

Surprisingly a lot of hunters do. I have about a dozen rigid or inflatable plastic decoys that hunters shot and tossed away as junk.

This inflatable plastic decoy has pellet holes mended with tire patches.

A large hole blasted in the side of this rigid plastic decoy was patched with fiberglass cloth. The cloth was left unsanded and rough to give a feather effect.

All have been repaired at little expense, and today they are admirably performing the duties for which they were designed.

Shot-damaged wooden blocks can be repaired with marine glue and wood filler. The wood filler can even be used to build up broken or misshapen bills and heads. Shot holes in rigid plastic decoys can be patched with the same fiberglass compound used for automobile body work. This compound can be purchased in inexpensive one-fourth-pint cans. Shot holes in some of the heavy-duty inflatable plastic decoys can be sealed with a hot soldering iron. If the hole is too large for this, it can be mended nicely with a wader or rubber boot repair kit.

The rigid plastic decoys are very susceptible to damage in portage, especially if they are lugged around in tow sacks. A dropped sack can result in cracked bodies, and then occasionally there is a character around who uses a sack of decoys for a seat. Again gaping holes and cracks don't mean a block is ready for the junk heap. These can be repaired with strips of fiberglass cloth and resin.

The life of a decoy doesn't depend solely upon its use in the field. One must also consider storage during the off-season.

Wooden blocks should be thoroughly washed and dried after the hunting season. Then stack them in the garage or attic where they will be free from moisture. If they are subjected to moisture during storage, they are certain to mildew. This can ruin paint finishes. Wooden blocks stacked under the old oak tree will deteriorate rapidly due to the weather elements. They will rot during the rainy season, and then during the summer the excessive heat will split bodies and heads.

Wash and dry rigid plastic decoys before storage. If they are left out under that same oak tree, seams are likely to crack in excessive heat. The least that can happen will be for paint to flake off. If these same blocks are stored in a damp place, the resulting mildew will ruin finishes.

Inflatable plastic decoys require the most care. They must be stored in a dry place that isn't subject to temperature extremes. By all means store them inflated. This keeps bodies filled out and lessens the possibility of bodies and heads folding in such a way as to cause creases, which in time will be the starting points for leaks. Inflatable rubber decoys should be only partially inflated in order to keep the insides of the decoys from sticking together. Inflation to the maximum is bad for it will keep bodies stretched to such an extent as to cause rubber fatigue. The least bit of moisture will cause rubber decoys to rot, so store them in a bone-dry place. It also helps to dust them with powder which will absorb any moisture that may collect. Most metal fittings attached to rubber decoys can be removed. Do so for the storage period, otherwise corrosion or rust may damage the rubber itself.

During the storage period make sure that anchor lines are detached from both the decoys and anchors. These lines are highly susceptible to rot at point of knot. Lines should be washed in warm, soapy water, dried completely, and then wound on a spool. They must, however, be tested for strength before being put to use again the following season.

It seems almost childish to have to mention decoy care and storage. Yet it is something overlooked by a vast army of hunters. I suppose they errantly believe that since the blocks are made to be used in water and under adverse weather conditions, they will stand weather extremes 365 days a year. It just isn't so.

23

Gimmicks

There isn't a sport going in which there are no gimmicks—devices allegedly invented or designed to give the user a special advantage over the nonuser. Decoying waterfowl is no exception. The gimmicks are there. A few work; most don't. The only common ground they have is that of separating the hunter from his hard-earned money. The devices are widely promoted before the season starts, and naturally some are sold. The users discover quickly that the contraptions really are not all they were touted to be. And the lives of these devices are short.

Some seasons back I hunted with a fellow who attempted to augment his spread with a motorized decoy. The decoy, nicely shaped and finished, had a motor in its body. A couple of flashlight batteries juiced the motor, which in turn drove a propeller. The decoy was attached to the anchor line by means of a bridle. In theory the thing was supposed to run around and around with the circle's diameter dependent upon the length of the anchor line. It worked as long as there was no wind and the water area was free of currents. With the wind up and currents running the motor was too weak to propel the decoy and the thing always ended up fouling its propeller in its own anchor line.

Even under ideal operating conditions I could never get excited about the device. To begin with lone ducks just don't go around swimming in circles. You will see ducks swim in circles only when a bunch of shovellers is involved. These ducks sift muddy water through their spatula-like bills. A characteristic of this species is for birds to follow each other when feeding. They swim bill submerged, sifting the muddy water churned up by the bird immediately in front. Eventually the lead bird turns in one direction or another, and inevitably a circle is completed in which the lead bird becomes just another follower feeding in the paddlings of the bird ahead of it. Shovellers, also called spoonies, go into this circular parade only on windless days and on dead calm water. If there is a wind blowing, they scrap the circle maneuver and instead work in a follow-the-leader line across the pond. Upon reaching the upwind shoreline, they flutter back downwind and recross the pond in a line again.

Shovellers are poor food fare because they feed so liberally on animal matter. Nevertheless they put on a first rate show in going through the feeding bit, and I get a lot of enjoyment just sitting in a blind and watching the performance. I let them hang around and await better ducks for shooting. I suppose in a way this could be viewed as using live decoys. It is legal, however, since the birds are wild and in no way tethered to the pond. It becomes illegal if tame birds specifically trained for the purpose are used.

If a fellow insists on using mechanical means to put action in his decoy spread, he should go to the dipper. There is a model marketed, but the method of operation is so simple that any hunter can rig the standard decoy to do the same thing.

A weight with a large ring-eye is placed on the pond bottom. Then a long line, tied at one end to the decoy, is run through the eye and to the hunting blind. The hunter actuates the decoy by pulling on the line. A sharp tug will cause the block to dip its head into the water as though it is dabbling for food. This device only works on hard-bottomed ponds where the weight is unlikely to sink and foul the line in the mud. It is a pretty good gimmick to use when the water is glass-slick. The tipping can cause sufficient ripples to make other decoys in the rig bob realistically. But I see no advantage in using it under rough water conditions or when the wind is strong. The elements then will give your decoy spread all the action it needs.

On several occasions I hunted geese with a fellow who used gimmick goose decoys. The decoys, full-bodied and handsomely painted, were balanced on metal rods which were stuck into the ground. The decoys were balanced in such a fashion that like a weathervane they would always face into the wind. On the few times I hunted with the fellow I never did get much decent shooting, and I suspect the reason was the decoys moved too unnaturally. They seemed to work okay in a light wind, but in a gusty blow their motion was unnaturally jerky. You know how a fishing plug wiggles when it is retrieved through the water? Well, those goose decoys did the same thing, only on a vastly exaggerated scale. I feel the geese reacted the way the congregation would to an Egyptian belly dancer performing in church.

Gimmicks are not by a long shot a modern phenomenon. There were a few back in the late 1880s. The most notable was a duck decoy with flapping wings. It was made and used on Lake Ontario around 1880 by a Capt. Charlie Do Ville. It was simply a wooden decoy with thin sheetmetal wings which were hinged to the body on springs. These wings flapped in the wind.

I dislike hunting a hard-bottomed pond where the water is clear and mirror-flat because both anchors and anchor lines may be visible to birds passing overhead. When I hunt such a pond, the first thing I do—and I do it in conjunction with setting out the decoys—is to shuffle around a lot to stir up sand to opaque the water. I repeat this on a limited scale each time I retrieve a downed bird. If you hunt the marshes, you won't have to do any mud-stirring. I have yet to see a marsh pond that was not muddy already. The crystal clear water is more likely to be found on the lakes.

One way to stir largemouth bass into feeding is to "plip" the surface of the water with a few BBs. The noise stirs the fish into feeding since it is remarkably similar to the sounds small minnows make when they break the surface of the water. The same trick can be used in waterfowl hunting, only substitute marble-size pebbles for the BBs. The sound is unimportant. When the pond is so still that the decoys look like they are glued on a mirror, you can break the stillness and ripple the surface by thumb-flipping out a pebble or two. The resulting ripples will make the decoys bob realistically. The main point to remember when using this trick is to refrain from flipping out pebbles in the face of decoying birds.

Feeder decoys can not be called true gimmicks, although many crusty old back baymen view them as such. It is understandable since they have no occasion to use them. Ducks, especially puddlers, do not go around feeding in rough water, and the water is more often rough than calm when it comes to bay shooting. Furthermore the feeder is out of character if the decoys are puddlers and used in water in excess of several feet deep. Diving ducks do not tip-up to feed. Instead they dive. So what is the point of attempting to rig a diver block as a tip-up?

The time and place must be right for use of the puddle duck feeder and tip-up blocks. The time is when the weather is serene and the pond is calm. The tip-ups especially will pendulum in ridiculous fashion in rough water. It is enough to send a self-respecting duck helter-skelter out of the territory. It is a sort of obscene version of the belly dancer mentioned earlier in this chapter. The place to use this puddle duck feeder decoy is in the shallow end of the pond.

That old dodge of a bird in hand is worth two in the bush has its parallel in decoying waterfowl, especially in connection with geese. It simply holds that one goose decoy is far, far better than none at all. It really is not a gimmick, but more of a trick in making the most of a characteristic of geese.

A single goose decoy in the field or on the water will not pull enough geese in range for the hunter to get a limit. But if this single decoy is spotted out late in the season, the odds are favorable that singles are likely to swing in close. In fact, there will even be times when a goose or two will actually decoy to the single goose block. Again with no means of communication with geese, we must look back to the habits of the birds for a possible explanation.

Geese mate for life. After a bird loses its mate it will do a lot of aimless flying, zig-zagging and criss-crossing areas seemingly in search of the lost mate. A number of old market hunters have told me that these birds are highly susceptible to decoying to the single decoy. The logical conclusion is that the loner may work to the single block on the assumption that it could be the lost mate.

Under no circumstances would I recommend the goose hunter to use but a single decoy. It is a good trick for the duck hunter to use. That single goose decoy in his duck rig can be most effective. It serves two purposes. One is that its presence can give suspicious ducks the impression that all is serene. Second it has that appeal to the lone goose seemingly searching out its lost mate. I have exploited the single goose decoy theory to some extent, and I have found it works reasonably well late in the season and particularly in areas when the gun pressure is heavy.

24

Easiest and Hardest

How easy or hard it is to decoy a given species of waterfowl varies tremendously. Some birds are hard to pull to the decoys whether there is any hunting pressure or not. Others, even in areas where the hunting pressure is heavy, are alarmingly easy to lure. One hunter will swear a mallard is harder to decoy than a pintail. Another waterfowler will argue the opposite.

Abundance of a species in a specific area is only a partial answer to the question. If mallards outnumber the pintails two to one, naturally the mallards will be easier to decoy. There are more of them. But there is more to it than that. Some species can be shot at many times a day and they will still decoy without the hunter having to make a lot of effort.

Consider the shoveller and redhead. As far as I am concerned one species is stupid, and the other possesses an addled mind. Ducks are supposed to be wary. They are supposed to circle and case the joint before joining the falsies on the pond. Not the shoveller. This beautifully colored but ungainly appearing fellow just comes gliding in to the blocks. If you refrain from shooting and just shoo it off, it is very likely to fly off a little distance, then turn around and return. Fortunately for this duck it is of such inferior table fare that most hunters refrain from popping it. If the shoveller was as succulent as the mallard, the species would probably be on the endangered list.

And then there's the addled redhead. This duck has to be crazy to land in the decoys when the hunters are plainly visible and making all sorts of commotion. Sometimes it takes a real effort to scare it off the water. It will raise its head high on its spindley neck and look at you like a fool.

In a marsh with tall, dense vegetation surrounding placid ponds,

This hunter has a bag of pintails, mallards, and a snow goose. They represent the easy and hard to decoy waterfowl. Pintails are extremely wary, while the snow goose is an easy bird to decoy.

I've found the mallard one of the easiest of all ducks to lure to decoys. Yet out in an open ricefield and even with a good spread of decoys, Mr. Greenhead can be a tough customer to pull to the blocks. He will often case your spread and then decoy to a bathtub-size pothole a hundred yards out of range.

On a big water slash in a marsh the wary pintail that decoys a hundred yards out of range is likely to stay there. This same bird reacts differently on an open bay. Even if it sets out of range, it will fiddle-faddle only a short time before it swims up to the decoys. I wish ducks could speak our tongue; I would like an explanation.

Take the gadwall, a species also known as the gray duck. Although this is a marsh duck, it is hesitant about working to decoys in a marsh. Yet out on the bay shore or in an expansive lake, the gadwall will make one or two circles out of range and then head for the decoys. Teal—blue-wings as well as green-wings—stool easy early in the morning, but they are tough customers to pull once the sun gets high.

Many waterfowlers say the canvasback is difficult to decoy. It is, if the hunter fails to take into consideration the decoying characteristics of this bird. It will sweep low and fast over the decoys, and then fly well upwind before making a turn. Then it is likely to make an extremely wide circle before returning. This takes time, and many hunters stand up in the blind to see where the birds are going. The birds see the movement and the hunter, and they just keep going. This is a case of the hunters making their own luck—all bad.

I bagged my first Canada goose some 25 years ago over a spread of snow goose decoys set in rice stubble. I spotted three geese off in the distance and started blowing my call. The birds angled in my direction and sailed right in to the decoys without making a single circle. I raised that nine pound double barrel. Bam! Bam! And I had my first honker. And, of course, I bragged how easy it was to lure Canada geese. I have bagged honkers since but never have they stooled so recklessly. If I had a five dollar bill—these are inflationary times—for every hunt on which honkers scrutinized the decoys and then set in a field a couple of hundred yards away, I could afford a few more of life's luxuries. For my money the Canada goose is the toughest of the goose clan to attract. In those sections of the nation where Canada geese are extremely plentiful there will be hunters who say the honker is easy to decoy.

The easiest goose to lure has got to be the lesser snow goose. I have had these dolts decoy countless times with hunters plainly visible in the rig. And at times smoking and loud talking no less. Yet just try stalking a gaggle of snows. When you are 99 yards away, they will take off. You can walk in plain view and these birds will pass directly overhead in easy gun range. But if you stop, look or point skyward, they will vector enough to pass out of range. As soon as ducks—except for the redhead—discover they are associating with phony clansmen made of wood or plastic, they are quick to skedaddle. Not old Sam Snow Goose. He will land in a spread of newspapers and stay. Frequently after getting quick limits of these birds I have stayed in the blind just to observe what succeeding flocks would do. I have had them come down in the phoniest of decoys and stay for as long as a half hour.

Based on my own hunting experiences, mostly in Texas and Lou-

This is a bag of four bluebills (scaup) and two green-winged teal (left). Both species work readily to decoys. Bluebills decoy best to diving duck rigs, while the teal come in best to puddle duck decoys.

These four shovellers winged over the decoys with the author standing in plain sight. They circled and came right back to set in the decoys. Shovellers are among the easiest of all duck species to decoy.

isiana, ease in decoying falls into three classes—(1) easiest, (2) moderately hard, and (3) hardest.

Taking the ducks first I place the following species in class 1: blue-winged teal, green-winged teal, cinnamon teal, shoveller, redhead, bluebill (lesser scaup), ring-necked duck and bufflehead. Class 2 includes: mallard, mottled duck, wood duck, gadwall, bluebill (greater scaup), and ruddy duck. Class 3 includes: black duck, pintail, canvasback, widgeon, and goldeneye.

Moving over to the geese, I put the snow goose and blue goose in class 1; the speckle-belly and cackling goose in class 2, and the Canada goose and Richardson's goose in class 3.

But whether the birds are easy or hard to pull to the blocks, there is nothing to compare with hunting waterfowl over decoys. It makes loss of sleep, numb fingers and toes, chapped lips and runny noses a small price to pay for the thrills involved.

25

Blinds

If a hunter is to harvest waterfowl consistently, the use of proper decoys is just the starter. Next he must have an adequate blind. The two—decoys and blind—go together like bread and butter. If you want to top this with a little "jelly jam" so to speak, then it should be done with the waterfowl call, which will be discussed in detail in a later chapter. These three items properly blended will pull ducks and geese into range consistently. If you fail to bag game then, it will be because you can't shoot worth a hoot.

Let's take a detailed look at blinds. Always keep in mind that a good spread of decoys will not compensate for an inadequate hide, and a good blind is of little value if there are no decoys to go with it.

A blind does not have to be elaborate to be effective. The real test of a good blind is in its being inconspicuous. It must blend in with the surrounding terrain. A blind can stand considerably above the adjacent vegetation if its shape is irregular so as to merge in as a grassy mound or small clump of brush. The same blind can become ineffective if its shape is out of character with the surrounding countryside. For example, the interior shape of a good blind is necessarily oblong if it is to accommodate more than one hunter. This shape, however, if it stands out clearly will certainly spook waterfowl. Consequently the geometric lines of a blind must be diffused with clumps of grass, brush, etc., spread around the outside.

This foliage arranged outside the blind should be done in such a manner that it will lean toward the center of the hide. This in effect provides a semi-canopy over the hide and will serve to disguise the geometric lines of the interior of the structure.

If this same blind is built out in the water, its general outline should be that of a small island. Again stay away from those straight lines and 90-degree corners. They can stick out like a sore thumb and cause suspicious birds to veer off.

A blind that looks good from ground level may appear like something else from duck and goose altitude. Consequently after a blind is constructed it behooves the builder to bum a ride in a light plane to scan the structure from a flying duck's point of view. After all this is the fellow you're trying to fool. Always keep in mind that a good part of success in waterfowl hunting is a fellow's ability to think like a duck or goose.

If hunters could remain completely motionless, there would really be no need for blinds as long as the fellows' clothing blended in with the surrounding vegetation. But remaining motionless is something very few hunters can do. Therefore blinds are a must. The back side of a hide must be higher than the front so the hunter's head and shoulders will not silhouette. Vegetation arranged at the rear of the blind should lean forward so as to partially roof the hunter. This will cast sufficient shadows for the hunter to get away with a reasonable amount of head turning without spooking the birds.

A good decoy spread with an adequate blind can be cancelled out if the blind's occupants are untidy. This means the area surrounding the hide should be free of spent shell casings, sandwich wrappers, etc. The sun can strike the brass of the empty shell hulls and cause them to shine. If the birds are already spooky, this extra winking is often enough to cause the ducks and geese to shy away before getting within effective gun range.

The good decoy and blind layout can be scuttled by careless or ignorant behavior on the part of the hunters within the blind. It goes without saying that one should not smoke when waterfowl are in the immediate vicinity. Smoke spells fire and fire to wildlife—whether mammal or bird—strikes total terror. When the birds begin to work the decoys, the hunter naturally must follow them as closely as possible. If he leans toward the front of the hide and looks through the covering vegetation instead of over it, he can get away with a reasonable amount of head moving. But if he sits well back in the blind, his face will be unscreened and it can stand out like a flashlight in the dark. This can be enough to vector the birds off and out of range and no amount of good looking decoys can salvage the situation.

Some forms of wildlife see colors only in varying shades of gray. This is true of almost all of the four-legged animals. Birds on the other hand can distinguish colors as such. If a blind is to be effective, the waterfowl's ability to recognize colors must always be kept in mind. A hide occupied by hunters wearing red coats and yellow caps is not going to be effective. This holds true even if the hunters have the ability to remain as motionless as death itself.

Any rich, vibrant colors that may be conspicious around a blind should be the hues that show on the drakes of the various duck species. In this particular case the colors should be on your decoys.

Where possible the hunter should avoid locating his blind in a place that would be between incoming birds and the decoys. Blinds can be so spotted, and one can enjoy successful shooting from them. But to get the most out of a blind so placed, the hide must be something extraordinary and unusually well camouflaged. Not only that, the hunter for considerable lengths of time will have to remain as motionless as a marble statue. This complete immobility is a skill few hunters have really acquired.

Always keep in mind that the very last thing you want approaching waterfowl to notice is the blind you occupy. It should be out of a bird's direct line of sight, and this certainly is not the case if the blind is spotted between the incoming birds and the decoys.

There is no such thing as placing decoys too close to the blind. For proof of this just thumb back into ancient books on waterfowl hunting and note the style that once prevailed along the Atlantic coast back in the days when sink-boxes and battery blinds were the style. The boxes had just a few inches of freeboard, and to keep water from slopping into the boxes, wings were built on all four sides. These wings served to break up choppy water. Decoys were placed on these wings and they were within spitting distance of the hunter himself. These boxes were low in the water and located a considerable distance from shore.

It is correct to place decoys close to a blind that is located on the shoreline, especially if the duck species sought are puddlers. These ducks are not at all shy about sidling up to a steep bank or even meandering under overhanging brush. On the other hand diving ducks are more persnickerty about close association with such things. They will approach close as long as there is open water ahead so as not to impede a run for that quick takeoff. Keep this in mind when spotting diver decoys like canvasbacks, redheads and bluebills near your blind. Just make sure that when they face into the wind, there is a long stretch of open water ahead.

26

Waterfowl Calls

A fellow, whether he is hunting ducks or geese, can have a fine spread of decoys, a good blind, and then ruin it all with lousy calling. If a hunter knows how and when to use a call, then he should by all means do so. It will reward him many fold. It will bring birds into close effective gun range and it will aid in cutting down on cripple losses. But if the fellow does not know how to use a call, he will find his hunting far more rewarding if he leaves the instrument at home. In the hands of an expert, the waterfowl call is a deadly hunting device. The same instrument in the hands of a tyro is a fine conservation piece. A waterfowl call used improperly will spook off birds long before they ever get in shotgun range.

Many duck and goose callers, even some of those skilled in making the proper calls in the correct sequences, are guilty of calling too frequently. They start off right, but they go too far. One of the secrets in effective waterfowl calling is knowing when to shut up. Initially the call should be used to turn the birds toward the decoys. After that it should be used sparingly. The general rule is that as long as the birds continue heading in the direction of the decoy rig, the hunter should do a minimum of calling. If additional calling is necessary, it should be undertaken only if the birds show signs of wavering or turning away from the decoys. Even then it should be done sparingly. Above all don't ever make that waterfowl call sound frantic.

Any hunter who thinks he can talk to the birds right up to the time when they hit the water is a fellow only fooling himself. When a guy sticks a waterfowl call in his mouth, more wrong than right things are likely to happen. And every time a wrong note or sequence is sounded, the incoming birds are further alerted that all may not be right. For the most part a few sour notes will not bother some species like bluebills, shovellers and redheads. Yet with other species like mallards, pintails, canvasbacks and especially black ducks, a single clinker note can turn incoming birds 180 degrees.

And then on top of that, even if no sour notes are sounded the incessant calling will serve to pinpoint the hunter to approaching birds. If the hunter makes suspicious moves or if he sticks out like a strawberry atop a mound of whipped cream, you can bet money the birds will swing away.

In order to use waterfowl calls properly one must know something of duck and goose calling characteristics. Ducks do most of their talking when they are on the ground or water. They make rather soft calls when they are heading into the decoys. The only time they are really noisy in flight is when they are alarmed. Then they quack loudly to the high heavens calling attention to all birds in hearing range that all is not right. Geese on the other hand are quite silent on the ground but are extremely talkative in the air. Correlated to waterfowl hunting this means the goose caller should use his call only to catch the attention of the birds and to turn them in the direction of his decoys. After that he should remain silent and let the decoys do the rest of the work.

In the case of ducks the caller should use the instrument to swing the birds to his decoys. As long as they are headed straight in, he should refrain from any calls except for occasional feeding chuckles. If the birds begin to wheel and circle, the hunter should resume calling every time they are turned away from him.

The cardinal sin in calling waterfowl is to sound the call after the birds—whether they are ducks or geese—have cupped their wings and dropped their feet. As long as the birds are in this attitude, they are coming down. Don't louse it all up by trying to add one last fancy toot on the call. Just ease your call out of the way and get ready to bang away when the birds glide into gun range.

Often, and especially in heavily gunned areas, waterfowl tend to decoy well outside of the rig. They will swing toward the decoys, fly the usual decoying patterns, and then go down on the water. But all this action takes place well outside of gun range. When this happens, you know you have a mighty spooky flock of birds on your hands. They are tired and obviously they want to come down to rest, but they have been shot at so recently and often that they will work only to wide open areas and well away from land masses. It can be most frustrating to have a flight of ducks work your decoys and then settle to the water a hundred yards away. In spite of some ammunition claims you are not going to kill any at that distance. If the birds are allowed to remain, they are almost certain to mess up your hunting since additional flights are likely to decoy to them rather than to your decoys.

If ducks are plentiful enough, the proper course to follow is to get up and chase the birds off the water. But do so without firing any shots. Yell at them or throw something at them. "Scare shots" with your gun will only chase them out of the county.

A different approach can be taken if birds happen to be scarce. If you remain still and well hidden, you may be able to entice the birds to swim into gun range. It will depend upon how realistic your decoys appear and how seductive you can be with the duck call. The proper call to use is the feeding chuckle. If your decoy rig happens to include a couple of feeder blocks, so much the better.

Ducks, especially mallards, are hoggish about feeding. They will feed and glut themselves to a point where they actually have difficulty flying. And all that is necessary to trigger the feeding binge are a couple of feeders and some seductive feeding chuckles. Those out-of-range birds will paddle in to join company.

You can learn to call waterfowl by taking lessons from professional guides or by studying any number of records available at sporting goods stores. You will note I have excluded waterfowl contest calls. The reason is personal; consequently it may or may not be valid. Nevertheless hear me out and then make up your own mind.

Contest callers do an excellent job of imitating the various calls, but most of them do so in a certain sequence. This is fine and dandy when the creature the caller is trying to impress happens to be another human. It is a horse of a different color when the waterfowl themselves are concerned. Ducks and geese don't always respond to a certain sequence of calls. The hunter must use his ears and listen for the sounds the birds are making on the day on which he is hunting. Then he should strive to imitate these sounds as closely as possible. And then there is one other thing about the contest callers. They are so in love with the sounds they make that they don't know when to shut up.

A great many waterfowl sounds—sequences, cadences, inflections, etc.—won't appear on duck and goose call records. They are sounds you will hear only in native waterfowl habitat. Okay, so how does one go about hearing these sounds? It is facetious to say "use your ears," but nothing else is necessary. Unfortunately few sportsmen really know how to use their ears. They depend far too much on these eyes.

There is a curious thing about nature. All forms of life possess various senses—sight, hearing, smell, touch, etc. Take away one sense, and almost immediately one or more of the remaining senses come into focus to compensate. For example, when you turn out the lights and walk from one side of a darkened room to the other, you subconsciously lean to the sense of touch for guidance. If on a dark night you happen to be in the wilds or some unfamiliar place, the sense of touch is augmented by still another sense, hearing. You listen for sounds, especially recognizable ones, that can give you a clue as to what lies ahead.

And so it is with the sounds that waterfowl make. Shut your eyes, and your ears will unlock wildlife treasures you never dreamed of. You can learn calls that will put you several cuts above your fellow duck hunters. You can learn tricks that will enable you to put game in the bag when other fellows don't even get to fire a shot.

Consider the weather that prevails on most waterfowl hunts. About 80 percent of the time there is rain, mist, fog, or haze to severely limit visibility. Tyro hunters think they can compensate for the lack of visibility by continually sounding the waterfowl call. That's so much hogwash. All these fellows do is chase the game out of the vicinity with their blasted sour notes. Yet if they knew how to use their ears, they would know how to call judiciously in order to be effective in pulling birds to their decoys.

First off there are the sounds made by the ducks and geese themselves. Imitate these sounds as closely as possible. Ah, but waterfowl made sounds other than vocal ones. There are their wings and the sounds they make in the sky. And on water the fowl make sounds, too, dabbling and swimming about. Just close your eyes, use your ears and you will hear a lot.

Let's just consider a few of these nonvocal noises.

Visualize this scene: The setting is the typical waterfowl marsh. You're hunkered well down in your blind, with a dozen and a half mallard decoys bobbing realistically on the two-acre pond. But there is a mist and ground fog. The visibility is reduced to something like a hundred yards. Not only that, it is such that even ducks flying directly overhead may not see your decoy rig. If you expect to get any shooting at all, your job will be one of using your call to bring the birds back for a closer look at the surroundings.

Let's disregard totally any vocal sounds the ducks may make. In this particular case we're going to concentrate exclusively on wing noises. Learn to recognize them and you will know when it is worthwhile to call and just which call to use. The wingbeat and how the wind whistles through the wings can clue you in on the probable attitude of the bird. In some cases it can actually identify the species.

A rapid whirring of wings can mean one of two things—badly frightened small ducks bent on getting the hell away from the area or curious teal, bluebills or baldpates. If the sound indicates the birds are flying in a straight line, don't bother calling them. They know where they are going. But if the sound of the wings indicates a curving or meandering path, use a subdued hail call followed by a series of feeding chuckles.

A slow, deliberate wingbeat belongs to a large duck like a mallard.

Use the same call procedures suggested for the teal, bluebill and baldpate wingbeats.

A strong, relatively fast wingbeat and one in which you can almost feel a beating of the air with each stroke of the wings belongs to a large duck species bent on flying to the next county. It is unlikely that you will be able to turn this bird. Unfortunately this same wing-beat is almost identical with that of some of the large diving duck species like the canvasback and redhead. Therefore while there is little hope of turning back an alarmed mallard, it won't hurt to sound some deep guttural "burrrs" just in case the wingbeat happens to belong to a diving duck.

Strong but irregular wingbeats belong to geese. If the sounds are coming toward your decoys or seem to be overhead, blow your goose call just enough to direct attention of the birds to the decoys. If the sounds appear to be going away, then get more insistent on the call.

This noise of the wings is not just so much jazz. It might sound that way, but if it does, it will be because you're guilty of not using your ears.

Just think back a little. Wing noises were quite evident to you in the dark of the pre-dawn as you made your way to the blind. Visibility was practically nil then and your ears went to work for you. Then came the dawn and light. The birds still made wing noises, but you bet all your blue chips on your eyes and allowed your ears to go to sleep. And then you wonder how that duck slipped in and out of the decoys without you having time to shoot.

You can prove the point to yourself by simply going into the wilds and putting on a blindfold. Don't just shut your eyes because you will be prone to peek and cheat. Tie the blindfold on tight and spend a couple of hours just listening. You will hear things you never heard before. Sounds like the watery rip of frightened minnows scurrying across the surface of the pond, the hollow grate and scratch as nutria gnaw cane, and the rustle of weeds as small predators approach the pond for water. And you will hear also a whale of a lot of sounds you can't identify.

Do this blindfold bit a few times, and you will stop calling that birdwatcher living down the street "some kind of a nut." You will learn new respect for that man's hobby. Odds are good you may become a "nutty wildlife sound listener," and you may even go to the birdwatcher to enlist his aid on identifying some of those sounds that seem so foreign.

It will all add new depth and meaning to your waterfowl calling. And then when you apply this knowledge to augment that spread of decoys on the pond, you will discover even more rewarding hunting.

27

The Proper Gun

A good spread of decoys, an adequate blind and skill with the duck and goose call will bring waterfowl into range, but without the correct weapon the hunter is not going to harvest much. The shotgun is the only legal firearm for waterfowl hunting. Shotguns come in various actions, a number of gauges and several chokes. All, however, are not suited for waterfowl hunting, and those that are may not do an adequate job for all types of waterfowling. Shotguns ranging from .410 (a caliber and not a gauge) on up to 10 gauge are legal pieces for waterfowl hunting. But legal and adequate are horses of different colors. Generally speaking and with good conservation in mind only shotguns in gauges from 10 through 20 should be legal for waterfowling.

Anything under 20 gauge is just too light. At best the 28 gauge and .410 bore are consistent cripplers and only occasional killers where ducks and geese are concerned. Yet even within what I consider the suitable range—10 through 20 gauge—common sense should rule out the extreme gauges on either side for certain types of duck and goose shooting. Specifically the 20-gauge is an excellent piece for over-the-decoys shooting, but it is inadequate for pass-shooting. The full-choke 10-gauge gun shooting 3½-inch magnum shells is a superb pass-shooting weapon if one has the shoulder to take the recoil punishment, but it is a horrible gun for decoy shooting when the majority of the shots are likely to be inside of 35 yards. At this relative short range this 10 gauge artillery will literally blow the birds to pieces.

Good shotguns cost a heap of money and not every waterfowler can afford two smoothbores—one for over-the-decoys work and a second for pass-shooting. So the hunter may well ask if there is such a thing as an all-round gauge that will serve both purposes. The answer is emphatically affirmative. Not only that, there are several types of actions available in this so called multi-purpose gauge.

This ideal gauge is the 12. Since many modern 12 gauges are chambered to take three-inch shells, they are excellent for pass-shooting. Even if the model is an old one chambered only for shells up to 2¾ inches, it is still a good long range gun since magnum loads can be used. This same gun, full choke, makes an ideal over-the-decoys weapon with high velocity and even standard low brass loads. The high velocity shells will fill the bill very nicely when ducks work to the outside of the decoy spread. The standard low brass loads serve adequately when the ducks work to the inside of the spread or at ranges under 40 yards. If the waterfowl are geese, this full-choke 12-gauge piece will serve admirably for decoy shooting with high velocity loads and for pass-shooting with the three-inch magnum shells.

So much for what is generally considered the ideal all-purpose waterfowl hunting gauge. Let's take a look at other sizes, starting with the 10-gauge.

This gauge gun chambered for 3½-inch magnum loads is far too much for normal shooting over decoys. It will kill clean, but those clean kills will be mighty messy if they are made inside of 35 yards. Anything inside is "blowup" range for this piece of artillery. This is a suitable decoy gun if a fellow hunts big open water and sets out a spread of several hundred blocks. A spread this large can force birds to work outside at long range. If it is necessary to use this gun for shorter range decoy work, then use high velocity loads instead of the magnums.

The 16-gauge shotgun appears to be slowly becoming obsolete. This is an in-between gun that does almost as much as a 12 gauge and just a little more than a 20. It is a good piece for decoy shooting but suitable only for moderate range pass-shooting. Since this gauge is no longer used by a lot of hunters, it is often difficult to get proper loads for the weapon. The loads are manufactured, but many sporting goods stores don't stock them since they are such slow-moving items.

Although I still occasionally use my 20 gauge for medium range pass-shooting, this weapon rightfully should be confined to decoy work only. The gauge, however, is excellent for hunting over decoys. It has maximum range out to about 50 yards and its ideal effective range is approximately 26 to 42 yards. This is the right gun for popping ducks at 20 to 25 yards, whereas a 12 gauge gun at the same range would hamburger the birds.

Shotgun bores come in varying degrees of choke. These include cylinder bore, improved cylinder, modified, improved modified and full choke. The choke determines the approximate percentage of pellets registered in a 30-inch circle at 40 yards. The full choke gun will score 65 to 75 percent of its load in the circle. The improved modified scores 55-65 percent, the modified is 45-55 percent, improved cylinder is 35-45 percent and cylinder bore is 25-35 percent. The denser the pattern in the circle, the better the odds of registering clean kills. Full choke, improved modified and modified are the only bores suitable for waterfowl hunting. Full should be used for pass-shooting and especially so with geese. Modified is the best bore for decoy shooting.

Two chokes can become instantly available only in the double barrel shotgun. Use the full choke barrel for pass-shooting. Use the modified barrel for the first shot over the decoys and then the full choke barrel for remaindering birds as they tower for the clouds. The single barrel gun can be made to serve both purposes by the installation of variable choke devices.

Each shotgun gauge and choke has its maximum range and its ideal effective range. The maximum range is the maximum at which a given load will kill. Ideal effective range is that range within which the pattern is dense enough for clean and consistent kills. Shooting high-velocity loads, the 12-gauge full-choke gun throwing No. 6 shot has a maximum range of 60 yards and an ideal effective range of 30 to 50 yards. The same gauge with modified choke has a maximum range of approximately 55 yards and an ideal effective range of 26 to 42 yards. The distances for the 16 gauge full choke are 55 yards maximum and 26 to 45 yards ideal effective. On the 16 gauge modified the figures are 50 yards maximum and 24 to 40 yards ideal. The 20-gauge full-choke gun with high velocity No. 6 load has an approximate maximum range of 50 yards and ideal effective range of 26 to 42 yards. The same gauge with modified boring has a 45-yard maximum and a 20- to 38-yard ideal effective range.

This brings us to the matter of shot size. What is right for pass-shooting may be totally unsuited for decoy work and vice versa. For example, No. 2 shot is fine for pass-shooting for it retains penetration energy out to approximately 90 yards, but this size shot is unsuited for close range work over decoys. No. 7½ shot is excellent for close range over-the-decoys shooting, but the pellets are so light that they retain insufficient energy to penetrate a heavy feathered duck or goose beyond 45 yards. If one wants a universal shot size to cover both pass-shooting and decoy work, No. 4 is an excellent choice. No. 6 shot is perfect for decoy shooting where the majority of the birds work within limits of ideal effective range. Shot in No. 7½ size will suffice on small ducks like teal when they work inside of 35 to 40 yards.

There is another shot size I favor for a specific purpose. The size is No. 8. The large number of pellets in the load provides a dense pattern for use on cripples. I call these loads "cripple stoppers."

When a crippled duck hunkers down low on the water with little more than head and neck showing, one needs a dense pattern to score a hit. Where geese are concerned No. 2 and 4 shot are ideal for moderate range decoy shots. No. 6 shot will suffice when the birds work in close.

Penetration and pattern determine shotgun ranges. Heavy shot like BB, No. 2 and No. 4 have the weight to retain kill penetration energy out to approximately 90 yards. Shell loaded with these sizes number 50, 90 and 135 pellets, respectively, to the ounce. As soon as these pellets leave the muzzle, they begin to spread out and the more the spread the poorer the pattern. In a 12 gauge full choke gun shooting a high velocity BB, 2 or 4 load the pattern density becomes inadequate beyond approximately 42 yards. This range can be increased by about five yards if magnum shells are used. An ounce of No. 6 shot numbers 225 pellets and fired through a full choke barrel gives an adequate pattern out to approximately 50 yards. But these pellets are small and lose velocity rapidly. No. 6 shot retains penetration energy out to about 70 yards.

The only way a waterfowler can stretch a given gun is to go to the heavy super loads, the magnums, the long three inchers and then the 3½ inch magnums. These super loads cost a lot of money, they punish one's shoulder and stretch the guns beyond decent range in decoy hunting. This book is all about hunting over decoys, so really what is the point of shooting super loads?

28

When to Shoot

When to shoot, whether it is pass-shooting or gunning over decoys, is always a problem. In the case of pass-shooting all shots are generally long ones, but when it comes to decoy hunting, the targets can be close, far off or in-between.

When ducks are scarce, a hunter has to be prepared to start shooting as soon as the birds get within range, even when the waterfowl may show signs of decoying. Too often these hints of decoying are simply moves made by the birds to rapidly lose altitude so that they can buzz across the spread for a close look. If the area is one in which the birds are scarce and hard to come by, then the hunter had better take his shots when the ducks zip across the decoys. If he allows the birds to make their buzz unmolested, he has no guarantee they have found everything to their liking so they will return. Too frequently they just keep going and fade into the distance. It can be disastrous if it is the only flock to come near that day.

The decoy hunter should wait out his shots in those areas where the birds are plentiful and especially so if a lot of them are flying. Note how these birds work the decoy spread and then act accordingly. If they consistently swing far outside the rig and come only into extreme gun range, then the gunner should try corrective measures. The proper action to take on open water such as a bay or big reservoir or lake is to move the decoys closer to the blind. The outside edge of the spread might not be more than 15 yards from the blind. On the other hand if the gunner is hunting a slash pond or relatively narrow body of water, he can spot his decoy spread near the far bank. This will cause the birds to fly down the middle of the neck between the decoy rig and blind, and this, of course, puts them in respectable shooting range.

The decision on when to shoot is most difficult when ducks are plentiful. Here the hunter fights within himself the desire to (1) shoot as soon as they get in range, (2) let them make a second pass at the rig, (3) let them make a third pass, and so forth. If this sounds ridiculous, it is only because a fellow does not have a lot of hunting experience under his belt. There are two kinds of waterfowl gunners— duck hunters and duck killers. The hunters are the ones who truly love the game they seek, and they are the folks who can get a world of enjoyment out of just watching the birds go through their decoying maneuvers. It sometimes gets to the point where they wait too long, and then there is the sound of firing two ponds away and off the birds go into the blue yonder.

This does not happen with the second group—the duck killers. They know exactly when to shoot and never let themselves be lulled into enjoying the decoying ballet. With the duck killers, it is killing pure and simple. Perhaps it is a sort of sex fixation with them.

There are times when the duck hunter must assume some of the instincts of the duck killer. When birds are scarce, the fellow can not afford to become mesmerized by decoying maneuvers. If he does, he may never fire a shot.

Now to go into the particulars of over-the-decoy shooting in areas where the game is plentiful. It can be to the hunter's advantage to pass up shooting at a couple or three early flights that may work to the decoys. Instead of concentrating on when to shoot these birds, pay strict attention as to how they work and what they do. A fellow can pick up a wealth of valuable information about the decoying habits of various species of ducks simply by being observant.

For example, the observant hunter will note that some species— like teal, bluebills and shovellers—usually come right in, often without so much as a preliminary pass to case the layout. It is not uncommon for teal to streak across a decoy spread full speed like they were heading for the next county. Then abruptly they wheel 180 degrees as a unit and drop down on the water. Other species like mallards and pintails will scrutinize an area thoroughly before cupping their wings. It is common for these species to make a half dozen or more circles in the area before dropping into gun range. These same mallards and pintails coming new into an area after a long migration flight will act in an entirely different manner. Usually they will glide down to the pond without so much as a single pass. This is most likely to happen immediately before and after the passage of a major weather front.

Then there is the gadwall or gray duck. This is a highly suspicious bird that cases a decoy layout by weaving figure eight patterns overhead. This bird invariably sets well outside the decoy spread, whereas other species, like mallards and teal, often drop onto a pond within just a few yards of the blind. I frequently have had these species work in so close that I had to wait for them to begin moving away before shooting. At extremely close range, anything inside of 20 yards with a full-choke 12-gauge gun, a shotgun blast centered on a duck or goose will tear it up beyond table fitness.

By refraining from shooting and by just observing how several flights work the spread, the hunter can get a good idea of how the birds are likely to work the rest of the day. The hunter may also discover that he can make flights work even better by relocating a few decoys.

When a flock of ducks or geese is working, keep tabs on the lead birds even when you know they will pass out of range. These are the birds that influence the reactions of all of the other birds in the flock. If the lead birds show signs of spooking, you can bet the remainder of the bunch will be just as edgy. Tail end birds can veer off, but unless they sound off with alarm "quacks" they won't influence the actions of the birds up ahead.

Particularly in the case of ducks a flight will often swing across a decoy rig in such a manner that the lead birds will be out of range but other birds farther back in the flock will corner their turn tighter and cross inside of long gun range. If the leading birds are satisfied that all is peaceful on the pond, they will continue to lose altitude and speed as they swing into a turn to circle back on the rig. This is fine. Let them make the swing and take your shots on the second pass.

But suppose the lead birds don't like the looks of things, and they begin to pour on the coal to vacate the area in a hurry? This is when the hunter should swing his attention from the leading birds to those in the flock that are in gun range. These birds are going to follow the pattern set by the birds up front, but their reactions are going to be a second or two after the leaders turn on their burst of speed or begin towering for the clouds. The delay is not much, but frequently it is just sufficient for an alert hunter to swing to an in-range bird and get off a telling shot.

Geese are different from ducks in that they never buzz decoy spreads. You can always hear geese coming. They call and talk all the time. Like ducks the geese are likely to wheel over the rig several times before coming down, but when they do decide to decoy, they come down rather slowly. Ducks on the other hand glide in swiftly and slam on their air breaks so to speak just a couple of seconds before they hit the water. Ducks make very few vocal sounds when decoying, but geese are extremely noisy. As a result, geese at the tail end of a flock can often turn the entire bunch away from the decoys.

I don't advocate pot shooting waterfowl on the water, although in all honesty my hunting experiences have not been without occasional on-the-water incidents. Nevertheless when ducks are plentiful in an area, it will often be to the hunter's advantage to allow ducks to land occasionally in the decoy rig. The hunter can learn a lot about his decoys by simply watching the reactions of the ducks on the water. If they leave in a hurry, just a few seconds after hitting the water, you can pretty well figure they found your decoys unrealistic or saw you. You know you have a good hide and excellent decoys when ducks land outside the rig and then swim back toward the spread. Don't expect this with geese, however, as they almost always stay put wherever they land. A lone goose setting outside a rig of goose decoys may swim over to join company, but don't expect this to happen with a flock of these big birds. If the goose decoys are in a field and the birds set down on the ground away from the spread, forget all about ever getting them to walk over to join company. Your best bet here is to allow the birds to remain unmolested and hope other flights will come in but decide to drop in with the decoys rather than the real birds.

When ducks make up their minds to decoy, cup their wings and drop their feet, they become easy targets. The first shot is strictly a "meat" one. If the hunter is interested in more sporting shots, he might try permitting the birds to land on the water, then frightening them and taking shots as they bound high into the air. This is particularly sporting with puddler species like mallards, black ducks, pintails, teal, etc. When frightened these birds rocket straight up into the air. Often that initial leap will send them 10 to 15 feet off the water before they head away in level flight. The shots are much like those on the flushing ringnecked pheasant, only the ducks can move about twice as fast as the ringnecks. The flushing-off-the-water shots at diving ducks is far less sporting or spectacular. The divers can only get airborne by rushing across the water paddling their feet and beating their wings. They resemble a seaplane building up speed to become airborne. The takeoff and flight path of a diving duck is predictable and easy to track.

It is a different story with the puddlers. Their spectacular leap off the water is straight up. It might be ten feet. It might be fifteen feet. Then there is the matter of direction in which the birds fly. The course can be any of the 360 degrees of the compass. Not only that some birds go into the tight climbing spirals and climb out of range in the matter of seconds. This offers some truly sporty shooting.

Several states went to the point system in determining daily limits in the 1970 waterfowl season. Under this system high point values are assigned duck species in short supply, while point values are low on plentiful species. For example, in Texas a hunter was allowed to collect 100 points of ducks a day. Depending upon the species involved he could collect a limit ranging from a low of two ducks to a high of ten birds.

Under the 1970 point system in Texas, a hen mallard was worth 90 points, a drake mallard 20 points, a hen pintail 20 and a drake pintail 10. All of these are good eating ducks, so there was little point in going for a 90 point hen mallard when a 10 point drake pintail would serve as well. Some folks had great difficulty trying to distinguish species on the wing. This is tough to do in dirty weather. So some fellows allowed the ducks to settle on the water so they could make positive identification. If the ducks were high pointers, they just allowed them to remain unmolested. In effect these birds acted as decoys to lure in more birds. These hunters went for the ten and twenty point birds so they could bring home a respectable number of ducks.

Shooting ducks on the water is not sporting. But allowing the ducks to land, flushing them and then shooting them on the rise is most sporting. It is much like jump-shooting but without all the tiresome walking involved going from pond to pond.

When to shoot, of course, involves first getting the birds inside maximum range and then into effective range. Keep in mind that maximum range in shotguns varies from gauge to gauge. Not only that, it varies according to whether the load is standard, high velocity or magnum. It does not stop there. Maximum range also varies according to the choke of the barrel. Obviously the first order of the day in waterfowl shooting, whether it is over decoys or pass-shooting, is for the hunter to know what his gun can and can't do.

The purpose of decoys is to pull waterfowl in close. If a hunter always starts shooting as soon as the birds move inside of maximum range, he is guilty of shooting far too soon. The exception, of course, comes when the gunner knows the birds will not work any closer. A waterfowler can also go to the other extreme. He can let the game work in too close. When you shoot at birds too close, one of two things is bound to happen. You chowder the bird to such a degree that it is not fit to eat, or you completely miss it. A duck inside of 15 yards is just too close for a full-choke 12-gauge gun. Better to take the bird when it is 25 yards out, and unless the hunter is skilled at dead centering every shot, it would be even wiser to take the shot at 30 or perhaps 35 yards. At 35 yards approximately 95 percent of the pellets in a load will be within a circle with a diameter of approximately 38 inches. At 30 yards the circle tightens to approximately 31 inches. At 25 yards the circle is down to 24 inches, and at 15 yards the diameter is reduced to approximately 13 inches. Obviously a fellow has to dead center his shots to hit at extremely close range, whereas out at 35 yards he can be a little off the target and still score a kill.

The ideal shot over decoys is one where the wind and sun are behind the gunner. A good wind blowing from behind the hunter means the birds will decoy straight into him, and with the sun behind him, it means odds will be slim that the birds will see the shooter from afar. Unfortunately not every hunt can be made under ideal climatic conditions.

When to shoot also involves whether the duck is coming or going. When possible going away shots ought to be avoided. Some will always be necessary since there will be times when few ducks work, and those that do will swing over the decoys and make knots going away in a hurry. Usually it will happen so quickly that the waterfowler will have to take a going away shot or no shot at all. Under more normal circumstances, however, waterfowlers should try to avoid this kind of shot since it is a game-waster.

It is not a really difficult shot. A fellow can score a lot of hits on going away birds, but clean kills are relatively uncommon. A duck or goose can take a lot of rear-end shot, be mortally hit, yet keep flying for a considerable distance. These rear-end shot birds bleed to death, but this generally happens only after the bird has flown a considerable distance. The hunter who can see a bird drop a quarter mile away in a thick marsh and then find that bird is indeed a rare fellow, one blessed with all the luck in the world. A bird so lost is poor conservation.

Waterfowl hit from the front or side go down quick. Vital organs get the least protection from feathers, muscle and bone when the pellets strike from the front or side. The head-on shot is an easy and deadly one. When birds come in from either side, the hunter should take them before they cross dead center in front of him. Remember after the waterfowl passes this point, the more they travel the more of a rear-end shot the hunter is forced to take. He will knock a lot of feathers out of the sky, but too many of his ducks and geese will fall out of reach many hundreds of yards away.

29
Collector's Items

A number of years back a friend who dearly loved to hunt ducks but who was in such a financial bind that he could not afford to buy decoys asked me to assist him in the matter. He figured I had connections to get him decoys at cost. I could have done just that, but realizing the depth of his financial troubles, I suggested instead that he walk the marshes bordering the bays around Galveston, Texas, after the duck season was over.

He was not quite sure whether I was serious or whether I was putting him on, but since I had given him some good tips in the past, he decided to take my advice. His Sunday morning jaunt was short, certainly not more than two miles. Nevertheless he found four wooden decoys. During the next two weeks he made four additional marsh hikes and ended up with a total of 34 decoys for the following season.

No, he did not steal the decoys. They were simply blocks that at some time during the season had broken loose from their anchors. High tides, strong winds and rough waters deposited them well up in the salt grass marshes where they became the property of the finder. If you happen to live in bay country where there is normally a lot of duck hunting, you can bet money the marsh grasses have plenty of stray blocks. All you need to do is look for them.

For example, there is a tremendous amount of duck hunting done on Galveston bays. One waterfowl biologist who used to fly aerial census counts over the bays told me that on a good hunting day decoys in rigs spotted over the bays probably number 10,000 blocks. One landowner who used to lease out blinds in the bay told me he put a rig of 100 decoys at each of his ten blinds. He put the blocks

Old waterfowl decoys often crop up in strange places. These were in a department store window dressing.

out the day before the season opened and left them there until the day after the season closed. He said he lost about ten percent of his decoys each year.

Now back to the fellow who ferreted out the blocks the tides had carried up into the marshes. Had he suspected that some of the old blocks carried considerable value, either as antiques or items for decorative purposes, he could have found enough buyers to solve part of his financial troubles. To make matters even worse is the fact that at the time I had not the slightest interest in anything antique.

Actually the serious waterfowler seeking to build up a huntable decoy rig will find it easier, cheaper and saner to go out and purchase popular models on the market today rather than to scrounge the back alleys, garages, attics and boathouses for hand-me-downs or to trudge the marshes for derelicts. Still if you happen upon an old decoy— especially if it is made of wood, canvas, or cork—check it out closely for value. Even if it bears no manufacturer's mark or symbol, it will probably bring a pretty good price from an antique dealer. And this goes for decoys that were made as recently as three or four decades back.

In doing research for this book I chanced upon an antique shop

This old wooden pintail block is not very realistic looking as far as a decoy is concerned. At the time of its manufacture some 50 years ago it sold for about 75 cents. Today it is something of a collector's item and in 1971 this decoy carried a $17.50 price tag in an antique shop.

This huge Canada goose decoy may be a poor imitation of the bird it is meant to lure, but today it has considerable value as an antique or to a collector. Before the turn of the century this decoy sold for one dollar. In 1971 it was listed in an antique shop at $40.

displaying several old and rather beat up decoys in its show window. I went into the shop and discovered several dozen more decoys stacked on shelves in the back. Two brands that were made as late as 1936 were priced at $17.50 each. Originally they sold for $15 a dozen. A cork and canvas mallard decoy reportedly made before the turn of the century was priced at $20, a straw-stuffed canvas pintail carried a $25 price tag, and a huge cork Canada goose decoy was listed for $40.

The fellow running across old decoys would do well to study the blocks and make strong efforts to determine their origin. The decoys, especially if they are hand-carved blocks from the Eastern Seaboard, could command quite a fortune from a collector.

Decoy making by machinery had its beginning shortly after the conclusion of the Civil War. The products that came out were known either as "factory decoys" or "gun store ducks." Although the bulk of the waterfowl hunting at the time was in the Atlantic Coast states, the duck decoy factories made their appearance in the Middle West. Detroit was the hub. The earliest and most famous of the "factory decoy" makers were the two Mason and Dodge plants, both located in Detroit. A third factory of equal importance was the Stevens factory in Weedsport, New York. All three factories made and sold decoys in huge lots. The prices ranged from $2.50 to $12 per dozen. It is interesting to note that while the bulk of the hunting was on the East Coast, the factory decoys sold almost exclusively in the Middle West and Southern states. The factories enjoyed little sales in the East, where waterfowlers seemed to look with disfavor on any decoy turned out by machinery. East Coast gunners had a fetish about their blocks. They wanted each decoy individually carved and individually painted.

According to various accounts of the times, waterfowl hunting was regarded more of a sport on the Atlantic Coast than in the Middle West or South. Market hunting was known and practiced on the Atlantic Coast, but apparently not to the extent that it was carried out in the latter two regions. The impression is that folks on the East Coast considered themselves quite a bit above their rougher cut brethern to the West and South.

Consequently the attics, barns and boat sheds of the Atlantic Coast are likely to yield decoys of unusual shapes, sizes and color schemes. These are the blocks that will bring fancy prices. Resurrected Mason, Dodge and Stevens decoys are more plentiful and considerably less valuable, although the prices they command are not to be sneezed at.

The waterfowler seriously interested in studying or collecting old decoys will find Joel Barber's book *Wild Fowl Decoys* most valuable. Published by Garden City Publishing Co., Inc., New York,

This pintail decoy is made of canvas stuffed with straw. The canvas was sealed against moisture first with white lead paint and then painted over to represent the species. Lower photo shows how the decoy is stitched shut.

in 1937, Barber's book is complete with numerous illustrations and drawings and is considered to be a textbook on the subject. I just wish I had run across this book back in the days when I started scrounging for decoys. It is just possible it could have enriched me considerably, for I came across a number of old decoys—solid wood bodies, hollow wood bodies, cork, cork and wood combination, cork and canvas and canvas and straw.

I disposed of those in what I considered to be too sorry a state to repair. The rest I refinished to suit my tastes, and in so doing I certainly must have desecrated some fine collector's items. This is a point that must be kept in mind more so today than in the past. There is a great demand for old decoys either as collector's items or interior decorative pieces for dens, offices and the like.

In connection with collector's item decoys, the Winchester Press in 1969 published *The Classic Decoy Series,* a portfolio of 24 color prints of paintings by American sporting painter Milton C. Weiler. In a move to honor a select group of waterfowlers who lifted decoy carving into the realm of pure American folk art, the Winchester Press commissioned Weiler to recreate in watercolor 24 of the most outstanding examples of the decoy maker's art. Each of the paintings is accompanied by a descriptive text by Ed Zern.

Works depicted include those of such decoy masters as Charles "Shang" Wheeler, Joseph Lincoln, Ira Hudson, Albert Laing, Capt. Ben Holly and Lem and Lee Dudley. If you happen to stray upon any blocks made by these master carvers, you will have a small fortune in your hands.

30

Call It Politicking

Waterfowl hunting is like a disease. Once the bug bites a fellow, he is infected with a disease that spans the remainder of his life. Each year as he grows older he threatens it will be his last season in the marshes, moaning that his legs and back muscles are not quite up to it. All this takes place about the middle of summer. Then right around the first part of September he starts checking over the decoys and mumbles things about making "just a couple of hunts this season."

The season comes. He buys shells—not by the box but by the case. Instead of a "couple of hunts" he goes every other morning. One becomes addicted to waterfowl hunting, and it is an addiction that ends only with the hunter's life. Early in the 1969 duck season an acquaintance, an avid duck hunter with almost 40 seasons of the sport under his belt, was found dead in his duck blind. He was the victim of a heart attack. Do you know how his duck hunting cronies reacted? Almost to the man each remarked: "He died happy."

With this outlook on the sport, it is only natural for newcomers to waterfowling to ask what they can do to insure the future of duck and goose hunting.

The obvious things are to play the game by the rules. Observe seasons, bag and possession limits, learn and master the capabilities of the shotgun, develop an ability to identify species on the wing, and strive to keep the loss of crippled birds at a minimum. These are things that tend to insure the immediate future of waterfowling.

Yes, the immediate future, which is next season, is important. Far more important, however—and especially if we expect to leave a waterfowl heritage for our children and then their children—are the seasons still decades into the future.

The length of seasons, the daily bag and possession limits are the

199

This Texas Parks and Wildlife Department photo is of a mixed flight of Canada, Hutchins, snow, and blue geese. The future of these birds stands in jeopardy as civilization continues to shrink wildlife domain.

results of supply and demand, that old tenet that makes the business world go around. We know the demands on waterfowl hunting are going to increase. This is only natural to expect in the face of the human population increase. How well the demands are met will be determined by how the supply is managed. This supply hinges on the availability of northern nesting grounds as waterfowl factories and southern resting grounds as wintering areas. Of the two the northern nesting grounds rank foremost.

No matter how realistic the decoys, how many one puts on the water, and how well one uses a duck call, you are not going to get any ducks if there are no ducks around. And you don't have to be on the hot desert sands for this to happen. It could take place right where you bagged those fat mallards and pintails and bluebills last season.

At this writing the prospect of no ducks sometime in the future is a distinct possibility: perhaps not in the next five years or in the next decade, and if you are as old as I am, perhaps not in our lifetime. Nevertheless it is a frightening possibility. Actually this chapter has nothing to do with decoys or decoying waterfowl, but it has everything to do with the future. If you are concerned with preserving waterfowl hunting for your children and your children's children,

The most plentiful geese today are the snows and blues. Smaller fowl above the geese in the photo are mallard and pintail ducks.

These are Canada geese silhouetted against an evening sky as they fly toward their roost. The Canada goose population is relatively low.

then this is indeed an important chapter. It concerns the legacy you leave.

If you so desire, call this chapter just plain politicking.

The old market hunter has been damned for his mass slaughter of game. But what he did awakened us to the dire consequences of his actions, and the market hunter was retired by law in 1918. At this writing, and for several years previous, duck stamp sales totaled a million and a half annually. The buyers bagged their share of ducks, and this harvest has had some effect on the overall duck population. If it did not, there would be no need for season, bag and possession regulations. If every duck stamp purchaser hunted—and bagged the limit—each day of the season, the results would be catastrophic. Fortunately about 75 percent of the buyers only get in two hunts per season, and their average bag is 2.5 ducks per hunt.

Hunters take their toll of game, but regulations keep it a normal within-bounds take.

The availability of game for the hunter's pot hinges on two things—breeding grounds and wintering areas. Almost all of the waterfowl available to the American hunter nests and breeds in Canada. Propagation depends upon the abundance of water. There is little we can do about regulating the amount of rainfall. There is, however, a lot that can be done about conserving the moisture that is available. Since the organization's formation in 1935, Ducks Unlimited, Inc., has done a tremendous job in this respect. This nonprofit group has poured millions into waterfowl factories in Canada, and roughly four out of every five ducks bagged in the United States come from DU projects. In spite of periodic droughts that affect Ducks Unlimited projects, the organization's work has been able to maintain some degree of stability in the overall duck population.

But after the birds leave Ducks Unlimited sanctuaries they are on their own. Dodging shot on their southward journey is a hazard they must endure annually. It is either that or stay in Canada and freeze into a solid block of ice. So then birds go south to ancestral wintering grounds. Many of these areas still exist, but not in the terms of what they were several decades ago.

The once tremendous waterfowl wintering marshes have been reduced to little more than isolated clusters of islands. The tentacles of civilization in the form of industrial and urban developments have snaked their way into the marshes. Dikes have been thrown up and the land filled. House, industry and streets checkerboard the areas on which wintering waterfowl frolicked. Ducks unfortunately can not fight back. They have no "quack" in the legislation that determines their lot. We can call the fire department when our house starts to go up in flames. The duck isn't so blessed. He can only take wing for the next marsh—and discover that it, too, has become a concrete and steel jungle. If he flies long enough, he will go well south of the border, and the Lord only knows what new plots he faces there. Still in those nations south of the line where education is minimal we can't lay the blame on the natives for what they do. Perhaps if they knew what the future might hold, they would change their ways.

If there is a fireman around to save the domain of Malcolm Mallard and Paul Pintail, it is the waterfowler, genus Americana, himself. Some real irony—the "killer" becomes the protector. Yet this is just what we face. If we are to continue to shotgun ducks and geese from the skies, we must be prepared to protect them as well. Today the major part of each dollar spent on duck stamps goes into the acquisition and operation of wetlands for duck nesting and wintering within the United States.

Unfortunately some refuges are initially too small. Others of some comparable size are having the ecology altered by urbanization and industrialization springing up around them. Pollution in some form drains off this civilization and contaminates the wild. In short, wherever man has been, his presence is felt. Too often what he has left is not good. A 10,000-acre refuge bordered by a ship channel on one side, a chemical plant on another, and an urban development on still another is not going to support as many wintering birds as the same size refuge located in a truly wilderness area. And what good is a refuge when the croplands for miles in all directions are turned into housing developments, airports and the like? If I had to drive 50 miles a day for my meals, I would quit my job and go elsewhere to work and live. And this is what the ducks are going to do, too.

Since the turn of the century we have seen the market hunter, spring shooting and live decoys become history, and the hand-tooled wooden decoy retired to the mantel. Unless we are careful duck hunting as we know it today could become but a printed page in history books of the future.

The individual hunter, whether he bags his waterfowl pass shooting, jump shooting, or over decoys, must learn to think in terms of not just what is good for him but what is good for all hunters. He must learn to discipline himself and reconcile himself to the fact that there will be seasons when the hunting restrictions in his flyway are much more severe than those in other flyways. He must understand the purpose of the flyway system.

We have four flyways—Atlantic, Mississippi, Central, and Pacific. They were established to provide flexibility in setting regulations. This system permits waterfowl managers to compensate for regional differences in waterfowl nesting, migration patterns and hunting pressures. Good waterfowl management seeks to direct the bulk of gun pressure against duck species in greatest supply, and limit—if necessary eliminate—the taking of species in poor supply. Success of this approach depends upon (1) hunter ability to identify species in flight, and (2) hunter willingness to forego shots at protected species.

The theory is sound. It works 100 percent at the conference table, but practical application in the field is something else. Too many hunters can't tell a duck from a crow unless the bird is in hand. And the only way you get the thing in hand is by shooting it. And then it is too late if the bird happens to belong to a protected species. Even worse there are those hunters who are downright cheats. When a million and a half duck stamps are sold annually, it is obvious there are not enough game wardens to go around to police the sport properly. You don't see wardens very often. In fact, in more than 30 years of waterfowling I have encountered game wardens only twice in the field.

In recent years "bonus seasons" were conducted in several flyways. The Mississippi and Central Flyways were permitted special seasons on early migrating teal, and three New England states were allowed a post-season shoot on black ducks. In 1967 in the two flyways, 165,000 waterfowlers bagged more than 450,000 teal, and the black duck season drew 7,000 hunters who dropped 28,000 birds. The teal bag in Louisiana alone that year was greater than the total bag of ducks in most states during the regular season.

Besides the number of hunters and birds bagged, did federal authorities learn anything of significance?

The answer lies in a news release prepared by Chuck Griffith of the Bureau of Sport Fisheries and Wildlife of the U. S. Department of Interior. In referring to the 1967 "bonus seasons," Griffith wrote:

"Poor hunter behavior was amply decumented during these bonus seasons. It was no surprise to find that some hunters couldn't tell a duck from a crow and that some hunters cheated. Nearly half of the hunting parties observed shot at protected species. Either these hunters couldn't identify illegal species or couldn't restrain themselves from shooting at them. Either way, the result was the same: too many protected ducks were killed and crippled."

A good many hunting camp managers refused to open their grounds for these "bonus seasons" for the reasons Griffith stated.

Joe Lagow of Anahuac, Texas manages the 19,000-acre Barrow Hunting Preserve. It is the oldest and most widely known waterfowl shooting preserve in Texas. Although it meant income out of his pocket, he refused to open the preserve to hunting during any of the special teal seasons. He told me the following:

"We lost too many protected ducks. Too many hunters can't tell one duck from another. The pass shooters are the worst. They shoot at any duck that flies, and sometimes they can't even identify a bird

*This Texas Parks and Wildlife Department photo was taken in the late 1940s
of a concentration of bluebills (scaup) wintering on the Texas lower coast.
Concentrations like this are hard to find now because so many wintering grounds
have become contaminated with various kinds of pollution or have been taken
over for waterfront lot developments.*

when they do have it in hand. Decoy hunters are much better, but
they, too, sometimes shoot protected birds."

The human element—hunting ability and hunter conduct—will
play a part in the quantity and quality of duck and goose hunting in
future years. When ability and conduct are improved, hunting regulations are likely to be liberalized.

I have up to this point in this book presented the facts about
decoying waterfowl. In this chapter I have taken the liberty to air
my opinions on the future. I hope I am wrong about the future. I
hope that a hundred years from now some fellow picks up this book,
reads it and then says: "That guy was all wet, predicting an end to
duck hunting. Why look we've got a ten-bird limit this season."

It is up to today's waterfowler to protect the decoy legacy handed
him by the old market gunners and tidelands sculptors, and in turn
hand down to tomorrow's children a legacy of good waterfowling
in their time.

31

Role of Migration

Ducks and geese travel on a north-south axis in the Northern Hemisphere. They head south in late summer to spend the winter in southern climes. When spring approaches they take wing again, this time flying 180 degrees in the opposite direction as they head northward to nest and raise their young. The cycle is called migration.

What duck and goose species a hunter is most likely to harvest in a given area depends upon which flyway that area happens to be in. Some species like the mallard and Canada goose are found in all four flyways. Other species may occur in only a single flyway. A hunter can use his decoys intelligently only if he knows the predominant waterfowl in his flyway. For example, it would be ridiculous to put out a spread of cinnamon teal decoys in the back waters of Chesapeake Bay. This bay happens to be in the Atlantic Flyway, while cinnamon teal are found common only in the Pacific Flyway and only rarely in flyways as far east as the Mississippi.

Ducks and geese common to each of the four waterfowl flyways in North America are listed at the end of this chapter. It can serve as a guide as to kinds of decoys to use.

Where a waterfowler happens to hunt within a flyway will determine to some degree how well birds will work to his decoys. Down in the areas where waterfowl spend the winter, hunters can get the birds to decoy to some rather decrepit blocks. This is because the birds are winter residents there so to speak and when they take to wing, it is only for short, local flights. The flight is unlikely to be more than a few miles from their roost to feeding grounds. Their urge for long travel has been temporarily satiated and won't be rekindled until well after the start of the new year.

The fellow hunting in states located between northern breeding grounds and southern wintering areas faces a more exacting situation. He gets the birds only as they pass through. Some years the birds make the trip in a hurry; other years they may tarry and loaf along the way. Either way the birds are restless with that urge to travel. If the waterfowler is to detain them for any time at all in this transit zone, he had better use good looking decoys. It is just as simple as all that.

Although this is the extent that migration plays in the art of using decoys to lure waterfowl, migration itself is a subject that never ceases to facinate people. It is often referred to as the promise of rebirth. Even though it has no key role in a book on decoying waterfowl, it deserves at least passing treatment.

Ever since Aristotle's era (384-322 B.C.) men with curious minds have observed bird migrations and sought to discover the reason for this curious seasonal activity. The number of theories then were legion. There appears to be no one answer, and today we still have several theories.

Real study of migration started about the time John James Audubon was engaged in his studies of North American birdlife. The practice of banding birds turned out to be the most direct method of proving the existence of migration. Results from bandings proved that most North American birds moved along a north-south axis. This happens to be a phenomenon mainly of the Northern Hemisphere. Studies further proved that while ducks and geese almost exclusively migrate north and south, only about 15 percent of the world's bird population that does migrate indulges in the north-south movement. East to west or vice versa movements are more common.

Banding led to the establishment of four main waterfowl migration paths in North America. Designated as the Atlantic, Mississippi, Central and Pacific flyways, the migration routes have become extremely important in waterfowl management and conservation. Additional studies of migration have proved that use of particular flyways by some species is hereditary. Some species of waterfowl trapped in one flyway and then released in another always manage to get back into the original flyway from which they were captured.

The "why" of waterfowl migration has not been absolutely explained to everyone's satisfaction. We know the birds come south for the winter and return north for the spring and summer. But exactly why we don't know.

It would be simple to explain that the ducks and geese head south when their northern nesting grounds freeze over and food becomes scarce. But this isn't exactly true. In truth migration from breeding areas starts long before winter arrives and at a time when food supplies are still plentiful. It is generally believed the rate of change in the length of days triggers some chemistry inside birds that are normally prone to migrate. In short it makes them restless. In the Northern Hemisphere the amount of sunlight varies between the longest day, June 21, and the shortest day, Dec. 21. Experiments show that birds' bodies are affected by sunlight, and it is the belief of many scientists that the effect of this sunlight on birds is what creates the urge to travel.

Waterfowl that arrive in the north early in the spring leave late in the summer for their southern migration. Studies made of these birds show that the length of the day the birds head north is about the same as the length of the day they start their southern migration. Since ducks and geese are sensitive to temperature, moisture, wind currents and light, it is highly possible all of these play some role in the chemistry of migration.

Okay, so we now have the birds down south. It would seem logical that they should want to remain south where the climate is temperate and food is always in plentiful supply. It was first believed that the return to the north each spring was purely instinctive. Some modern biologists, however, support the theory that the return north may be based more on logic than instinct. The basis for this theory is that rich insect life (common waterfowl fodder) abounds with relatively few predators on the northern nesting grounds. These same biologists contend that if the migrants remained in the south, they would have too many other creatures to compete with during the important breeding, nesting and rearing period.

The fact that the word "logic" is used tends to indicate waterfowl have sufficient brain development in order to think and reason.

There is still another factor to be considered in the desire to return north. It is just plain old sex, that three-letter word that makes everything in the world go round and round. In 1925 William Rowan found through experiments that the change in the length of daylight, controlled to correspond directly with migration time in the spring, triggered migration through sexual stimulus.

When it comes to celestial navigation, man may not have been the first to employ it. Waterfowl do most of their migrating at night, and experiments have proved that the birds use the stars in orienting themselves. All waterfowl navigation, however, may not be based on the stellar system.

Some scientists place stock in the earth's magnetic field. They contend the birds sense magnetic deviation and pull. In short, the idea suggests waterfowl may have built-in compasses.

Still other biologists lean to the contention that in the case of geese the migration route is handed down from parent to offspring. This would suggest the long trip south in the fall and the equally long return in the spring are made by visual navigation. Since geese do much of their migrating at night, this would suggest the birds have uncanny visual skills Although migrating flights of geese have been sighted by airline pilots at altitudes of 10,000 to 12,000 feet, the more normal migration altitude is around 2,000 feet. From this height one can make out landmarks at a distance of 65 miles. But this is possible only on a clear day. Of all the theories advanced to support migration, the one based on visual navigation is the weakest.

The waterfowl flyways reading from east to west across the Northern Hemisphere are Atlantic, Mississippi, Central and Pacific.

The Atlantic Flyway has its roots in Greenland, the northern parts of the eastern Canadian provinces and New England. This flyway generally follows the Atlantic Coast, and waterfowl in it take this route to Florida, Cuba and South America.

Adjacent to it and immediately to the west is the Mississippi Flyway. Its roots stem mainly from the central portion of Canada and the Northwest Territories. It runs along the Great Lakes and down the Mississippi River Valley to the Gulf of Mexico. From there the birds swing to Cuba and Central America.

The roots of the Central Flyway are found mainly in northwestern Canada and the Northwest Territories. One root has its beginning in the northern tier of the Midwestern United States. This flyway generally follows the line of the Rocky Mountains with a strong leaning toward the Texas coast. Birds from this flyway go into Mexico and Central America.

The most westerly flyway is the Pacific. Although one of its roots begins in the Bear River Marshes in Utah, its basal roots are found in westernmost Canada and Alaska. Birds using this flyway follow the Pacific Coast on their migration to Mexico and Central America.

Now to the listing of waterfowl commonly found in each of the flyways. Species are not listed in a flyway if their appearance is only occasional or rare. For example, the mottled duck appears in the Atlantic Flyway only in Florida and in the Central Flyway only in Texas, but they are plentiful enough in both of these flyways to be included in the listings. There is little point in fooling with the Mexican duck, which is sometimes referred to as the Mexican squealer because its range is restricted to a very small portion of the southwest in the Central Flyway.

ATLANTIC FLYWAY

DUCKS: mallard, black duck, gadwall, widgeon, pintail, green-winged teal, blue-winged teal, wood duck, shoveller, ruddy duck, redhead, canvasback, greater scaup, lesser scaup, ring-necked duck, common goldeneye, bufflehead, common merganser, red-breasted merquin duck, white-winged scoter, surf scoter, common scoter, common eider, king eider, spectacled eider, common merganser, red-breasted merganser, hooded merganser.

GEESE: Canada and sub-species, greater snow, American brant.

MISSISSIPPI FLYWAY

DUCKS: mallard, black duck, gadwall, widgeon, pintail, green-winged teal, blue-winged teal, shoveller, wood duck, ruddy duck, redhead, canvasback, greater scaup, lesser scaup, ring-necked duck, common goldeneye, bufflehead, common merganser, red-breasted merganser, hooded merganser.

GEESE: Canada and sub-species, white-fronted, lesser snow, blue.

CENTRAL FLYWAY

DUCKS: mallard, black duck, pintail, mottled duck, gadwall, widgeon, green-winged teal, blue-winged teal, shoveller, wood duck, ruddy duck, redhead, canvasback, ring-necked duck, lesser scaup, common goldeneye, bufflehead, common merganser, red-breasted merganser, hooded merganser.

GEESE: Canada and sub-species, white-fronted, lesser snow, blue.

PACIFIC FLYWAY

DUCKS: mallard, pintail, gadwall, widgeon, green-winged teal, blue-winged teal, cinnamon teal, shoveller, wood duck, ruddy duck, redhead, canvasback, ringnecked duck, greater scaup, lesser scaup, common goldeneye, Barrow's goldeneye, bufflehead, old squaw, harlequin duck, white-winged scoter, surf scoter, common scoter, Steller's eider (Alaska only), king eider (Alaska only), common merganser, red-breasted merganser, hooded merganser.

GEESE: Canada and sub-species, black brant, white-fronted, lesser snow, blue, emperor (Alaska only).

Migration flights are most dramatic at points of origin, and especially where geese are involved. Most of the geese—the Canadas and sub-species, snows and blues—leave their northern breeding grounds and travel in groups of several families to James Bay, which is located adjacent to and south of Hudson Bay. James Bay extends well down between the Canadian provinces of Quebec and Ontario. James Bay is the assembly point of these geese just prior to winging southward to their wintering grounds. The concentrations build up on James Bay the way the Allies did in England in preparation for D-Day on Normandy beaches. The birds spend but a short time in the James Bay region, and then wend southward in concentrations of almost unbelievable numbers. Their formations of V's and lines in the sky make living and ever changing lacework patterns of fantastic beauty. And all the time their calls ring out almost to the horizon.

Duck migrations are far less spectacular for they migrate in far smaller concentrations and do so almost exclusively at night. Furthermore the ducks follow more meandering paths, dodging well around islands of civilization that may lie in their paths. Geese on the other hand will just gain altitude and fly directly over cities and densely populated areas. It is truly a sight to behold—the wild and the civilized in sight of each other and each going its own way.

Galveston, Texas, where I live is on the fringe of what was once a vast ancestral wintering grounds for millions and millions of waterfowl. I hunt ducks and geese at every opportunity, but my interest in waterfowl does not stop when the shooting season ends. One of the most interesting observations after each season is that of keeping tabs on the buildup of snow goose concentrations as the birds begin preparing for their return north. It is easy to keep track of these birds because their large size and white color makes them so conspicuous.

These geese invariably depart from their Texas wintering grounds in March, with the actual leaving coinciding with full moon. The geese begin banding together more and more as the full moon period approaches, and the concentrations are so huge that from a distance the fields appear white with snow. The closer the full moon approaches, the more restless the birds become.

And then when the full moon arrives, the birds begin winging northward. The actual leaving always starts late one afternoon and right around dusk. It continues all night. Flight after flight take wing and head north with the birds doing a great amount of talking. Only their spring talk is far different from that heard in the fall. In the fall and throughout the winter, the call of the wild goose is rather drawn out. That heard in the spring is a chatter. The departure of snow geese is not all done in a single night. It spans over a period of three to four nights. Then the fields that were once white with geese are back to their normal blacks and browns and greens. All that remains to give evidence that geese were once there are droppings and a few feathers.

On their northern journey, the geese climb to great heights in a considerable hurry. Usually they fly all night and don't descend until daylight of the following day. And then it is mainly to feed. The journey northward is made at a leisurely pace with set-downs of a few days each in just about every state between Texas and the Canadian border. Stops for feeding are also made in the wheatfields of the Canadian provinces. How long the birds tarry at each stop depends upon the availability of food. The pace of the northern migration is slower than that of the southern flight made in the fall of the year.

The birds get to their nesting grounds on the tundra in the Arctic

Circle early in May. They breed and begin their nesting by the middle of May.

These same birds return to their Texas wintering grounds in October, with their arrival timed to coincide with the full moon again.

32

Those Provincial Names

If distribution of this book was limited to the three counties that make up the upper Texas coast, there would be no need for this chapter. The natives of these counties know the various ducks and geese by the names used throughout the text.

Names given to the various species of waterfowl are like the names applied to fish species—they vary from one section of the country to another. It would be great if a species had its scientific name, a common name and then stop right there. But people are more provincial than cosmopolitan. They are proud of the sections of the nation from which they come, and they cling to the colloquial phrases, habits and so forth. This is good. After all few people would really enjoy living in a completely regimented society.

Throughout this book I have referred to ducks and geese by their most generally accepted common names. Unfortunately in the case of some birds the common names may be completely "foreign" in some sections of the nation or to a certain breed of hunters. A good example is the pintail duck. Pintail is the common name for the bird the waterfowl biologist knows as Anas acuta. Back in the days of the market hunter, the old mossback meat hunters on the Texas coast called it a "sprig" and nothing else. A long deceased uncle who did his share of market gunning in his day often told me. "Only city slickers call it a pintail. It's a sprig. Now you remember that now!"

Folks along the east coast call Aythya marila and Aythya affinis greater scaup and lesser scaup, respectively. Only since the establishment and growth of the National Aeronautics and Space Administration (NASA) complex near Houston, Texas, has the name scaup come into use along the Texas coast. Prior to the migration of east coast scientists, many of whom like waterfowl hunting, the scaup was called a bluebill by native Texans.

Some of our ducks and geese have only three or four provincial names. Others may have scores of colloquial names. The ruddy duck is a good example. This comical little bird has at least 30 accepted provincial names. It is interesting to note that this bird with so many names is not often sought by hunters. I believe this bird has so many names because of the attention it attracts by its various antics. The ruddy duck is best described as a comical duck. It is as much at home on the water as under it. It dislikes leaving the water and seems to prefer escaping by diving rather than flying. It is a crazy duck that will stay on a pond even when hunters are shooting at it. It seems to have a sort of sixth sense that causes it to dive just a split fraction of a second before a hunter pulls the trigger. The ruddy duck can dive and vanish in a flash, or like the grebes it can slowly sink out of sight like a submerging submarine.

There are times when a new name catches with a certain species and with it comes new respect for the bird. Snow and blue geese offer excellent examples. In the days of market hunting these geese were called white and gray brant, respectively. Not only that the old market hunters of the South regarded these birds as "trash geese." I recall the tales spun by many of the old market gunners. They considered shooting snow and blue geese as a waste of shells. They wanted only the choice Canada goose and speckle-belly. Canadas and specks are hard to come by in many sections of the land these days, and as a result snow and blue geese have more respectable reputations today. Not only that, one only rarely hears the names white and gray brant used any more in the south. I suppose when the last of the market hunters dies these names will vanish, too.

The mass of provincial names is the reason for this chapter. In each case the common name is listed first, then the scientific name in parenthesis with the provincial names following.

DUCKS

MALLARD (Anas platyrhynchos) : greenhead, northern mallard, winter mallard, English duck, stock duck, barnyard duck, wild duck.

BLACK DUCK (Anas rubripes tristis) : black mallard, dusky mallard, dusky duck, summer black duck, blackie.

REDLEGGED BLACK DUCK (Anas rubripes rubripes) : red-leg, winter black duck, redleg black mallard, clam duck.

MOTTLED DUCK (Anas fulvigula) : Texas mallard, summer mallard, southern mallard, summer black duck.

PINTAIL (Anas Acuta) : sprig, spiketail, longneck, gray duck, bay duck, sea widgeon, picket-tail, pheasant duck.

GADWALL (Anas strepera) : gray duck, gaddy, gray widgeon, speckle-belly duck, creek duck, marsh duck.

AMERICAN WIDGEON (Mareca americana) : baldpate, widgeon, blue-billed widgeon, whistler, poacher duck, green-headed widgeon, southern widgeon, California widgeon, white-face, baldhead.

BLUE-WINGED TEAL (Anas discors) : teal, blue teal, summer teal, blue-wing, big teal.

GREEN-WINGED TEAL (Anas carolinensis) : teal, common teal, redhead teal, green streak, green-wing, mud teal.

SHOVELLER (Spatula clypeata) : spoonbill, spoonie, broadbill, shovel-bill, marsh greenhead.

WOOD DUCK (Aix sponsa) : woody, summer duck, squealer, tree duck, wood widgeon, acorn duck.

REDHEAD (Aythya americana) : fiddler, red-headed bluebill, bay duck, fool duck, American pochard, raft duck.

CANVASBACK (Aythya valisineria) : can, white-back, bullneck, wedge-head.

RING-NECKED DUCK (Aythya collaris) : ringbill, blackjack, pond bluebill, blackhead, ring-necked scaup.

LESSER SCAUP (Aythya affinis) : blackhead, bluebill, broadbill, bay duck, raft duck, river bluebill, creek broadbill.

GREATER SCAUP (Aythya marila) : same provincial names as those applied to the lesser scaup.

GOLDENEYE (Bucephala clangula) : whistler, tree duck, wood duck, copperhead, brass-eye, great-head, garrot.

BUFFLEHEAD (Bucephala albeola) : butterball, dipper, spirit duck, dapper duck.

RUDDY DUCK (Oxyura jamaicenis) : butterball, broadbill, black-jack, bluebill, daub duck, dipper, dapper, broadbill diver, creek coot, pond coot, dumbhead duck, goose widgeon, fantail duck, stiff-tail, spike-tail, bumblebee coot, hardhead, tough-head, sleepyhead, booby, murre, gray teal, salt-water teal, spoonbill pintail, shot pouch.

GEESE

CANADA GOOSE (Branta canadensis) : Canadian, Canadian honker, bay goose, ring-neck, black-necked, white-cheeked goose, wild goose, long-necked goose.

WHITE-FRONTED GOOSE (Anser albifrons) : speckle-belly, laughing goose, gray wavy, gray brant, yellow-legged goose.

SNOW GOOSE (Chen hyperborea) : brant, white brant, white wavy, winter goose, white goose.

BLUE GOOSE (Chen caerulescens) : brant, blue brant, gray brant, blue wavy, blue snow goose, blue-winged goose.

MERGANSERS

COMMON MERGANSER (Mergus merganser) : fish duck, sawbill, goosander, American merganser, buff-breasted merganser, sheldrake, pond sheldrake, swamp sheldrake, breakhorn, bracket sheldrake.

RED-BREASTED MERGANSER (Mergus serrator) : hairy-head, sheldrake, fish duck, sawbill, salt water sheldrake, shell-bird, fish-eater, sea robin.

HOODED MERGANSER (Lophodytes cucullatus) : sawbill, fuzzyhead, wood sheldrake, pond sheldrake, spike-bill, hairy-crown, sawbill diver, pickaxe sheldrake, water pheasant, hooded sheldrake.

Appendices

APPENDIX 1. WATERFOWL PHOTOGRAPHY

The United States entered the 1970s with its attention focused sharply on environment and ecology. Some dire predictions have been made that man may pollute himself out of existence in the 21st century. The talk has served two purposes. A substantial part of our population is striving toward cleaning up its own filth. Along with this primary move, there is a secondary one. It is a renewal of man's interest in the wildlife world for he realizes that he may be able to make amends to prolong Homo sapiens's existence on this planet, but he is not too sure he can do the same for our wildlife.

As the population continues to expand, so does the spread of civilization with its ubiquitous mantle of concrete, asphalt and steel. Like the flow of lava from the angered volcano and the swelling tide of the rampant hurricane, civilization's growing urbias and suburbias are shrinking wildlife's habitat. In this respect a surprisingly large number of people are showing an interest in wildlife, not as hunters, but strictly as observers. The bulk of them are birdwatchers. Many of these birdwatchers augment their hobby with photography, and it is in this connection that this appendix is written.

The problem in waterfowl photography is identical with that in hunting—a matter of getting the game within effective range of the instruments used. In this respect the waterfowl decoy can serve as the attraction to lure the birds. These decoys used in connection with a good hide and adequate photographic equipment can net the observer some treasured photos.

The waterfowl photographer is not bothered with a season, bag or possession limits. The only restrictions placed on him are his ingenuity and stealth in getting close to his subjects and the limitations of his equipment.

The standard in waterfowl photography today is the single lens reflex camera. The user points the camera, focuses it and then snaps the shutter. He gets exactly what he sees in the viewer, for through a system of mirrors, he is viewing the subject through the lens. This camera is small and fast working. It allows the use of telephoto lenses without adding cumbersome focusing or viewing devices.

An absolute essential in this kind of photography is a telephoto lens, and up to a point, the more powerful the magnification, the better. Lens magnification is in direct relation to its focal length. In today's 35mm cameras, the most popular size for single lens reflex (SLR) models, a lens with a focal length of 50mm is considered normal. Lenses with longer focal lengths are then telephoto; those with shorter focal lengths are wide angle. The minimum for waterfowl photography with a 35mm camera is a 200mm lens, which will record an image four times larger than the 50mm lens. The waterfowl photographer, however, will find either a 300mm or 400mm lens more practical. At today's prices excellent 200mm or 400mm lenses can be obtained in a price range of $200 to $300. If these prices are too steep, considerable savings can be realized by shopping around for used lenses of the same make, or if one can live within certain limitations, some of the economy priced telephoto lenses in the $100 category will suffice. At some aperture openings, some of the economy lenses will produce results equal to that of the more expensive lines. Actually photographs taken by the two lenses are hard to tell apart unless they are enlarged to extreme proportions like 18 x 20 or bigger. If enlarged to the usual 8 x 10 size only a professional can distinguish any difference.

When one starts using lenses over 300mm, the gain in image size is often costly. The least bit of camera movement or vibration will show up as a blur in the photo. If one does not have a steady hand, then a good tripod is necessary. If shooting sessions require long hours, then a tripod is a must. The tripod should have a pan head that can be moved on both vertical and horizontal axes.

Waterfowl at rest are easiest to film. The photographer has the time to get needle sharp focus and he can steady his camera. The next easiest photos are "flock shots." These are pictures of large masses of flying birds, and the bigger the concentrations the easier the pictures. Just stop the camera down to its smallest aperture to get as much depth of field as possible.

The most difficult photos are those of one or two birds in flight. You want to get as sharp a focus as possible to capture every detail on the bird, but a moving bird is difficult to keep in focus, especially when a telephoto lens is involved. To get consistently good results any of several techniques can be employed. To begin with, in filming the flying duck or goose the photographer is naturally moving his camera to keep the bird in the view finder. It is most important that he keep panning the camera and follow through during the shutter snapping. The background, of course, will be blurred due to camera movement. But look what happens if you stop the camera to trip the shutter. The background is sharp, but the flying bird is blurred.

The second technique involves being familiar with landmarks. This is particularly helpful if the ducks and geese are flying low enough so that part of the terrain appears in the view finder. Make a list of the landmarks—trees, bushes, etc.—that stand out. Focus the camera sharply on each object and mark down on a list the distances noted on the lens scale. When a duck or goose flies in such a direction that it will come within range of the camera, all the photographer needs to do is anticipate its flight path. Then he can note on his chart the distance to the tree, bush or shoreline the bird will fly over shortly and pre-set his lens on the correct focus.

Still another method is to set the lens for a certain distance, pick up the bird in the view finder and follow it along until it looms clear and distinct. It is then in focus and all the photographer needs to do is trip the shutter.

Decoys can lure waterfowl in close enough for some dramatic photographs. The photographer can get those photos of water droplets falling off the duck's bill. The decoys will lure the birds close enough. His big problem is to make as little noise and movement as possible as he operates his photographic equipment.

APPENDIX 2.   DECOYING DOVES AND CROWS

Mention decoys and immediately one associates the word with waterfowl. To the uninitiated as well as a number of reasonably knowledgeable hunters no other creatures other than ducks and geese come to mind when the subject of decoys is broached. Prior to the turn of the century the decoy was used for a number of shorebirds in addition to ducks and geese. To the hunter, circa 1900, the word decoy would have brought to mind ducks, geese, egrets, herons, snipe, cranes, and sand pipers to mention just a few. But as various bird species declined in population, the use of decoys for these creatures was legislated into limbo.

So today the vast majority of outdoorsmen think of decoys only in terms of hunting waterfowl. To a lesser extent, however, decoys are popular items in North America for two other bird species and—don't laugh—fish. It really should not take any imagination to realize that the fishing lure that wiggles and wobbles through the water is actually nothing more than a decoy to attract fish.

The purpose here is not to digress into the realm of attracting fish with lures. If the reader is so inclined to pursue this subject, the author of this book covers artificial lure fishing in depth and detail in his book *Lure Fishing* published by A. S. Barnes & Co., Inc., in 1970.

The intent in this appendix is to point up very briefly modern day use of decoys for birds other than waterfowl. The cases concern doves and crows. Whereas approximately 90 percent of the waterfowl hunters use decoys to some degree to lure their ducks and geese, less than 10 percent of the dove hunters bother to augment their hunts with decoys. In the case of crow hunters, approximately 60 to 75 percent of them resort to decoys.

Doves are gregarious birds, and they work to decoys simply because they love company. Unfortunately two factors work against widespread use of dove decoys. To begin with the bird is predominantly gray in color and this in itself is excellent camouflage. At any distance at all doves are difficult to see against a fall or winter sky. Perched doves stand out only if they are on the naked limbs of a dead tree, on telephone and power lines or on the strands of a barbed wire fence. If doves rest in foliaged trees, one will never see the birds until they flush. This, then, rules out using dove decoys in most trees. Rigging the decoys on the limbs of a dead tree is difficult because of the climbing necessary. It goes without saying that decoys should never be rigged on either telephone or power lines. Decoys spotted on fence rails are difficult for high flying birds to see. Furthermore doves that do drop to the decoys on the fence can lead to shots that can get the unobservant hunter into trouble. Often these low shots put grazing livestock, and sometimes other hunters, in the line of fire.

Two different kinds of decoys are used in crow hunting. One is to put out a number of crow decoys all arranged in one tree so as to suggest a roost or rallying point. A half dozen to a dozen will suffice. The second is to rig an owl decoy high in a tree. Crows love to gang up on this bird of prey. Whether the owl or the crow decoys are employed, either rig to be really effective must be augmented with a crow call to attract attention.

APPENDIX 3. TRANSPORTATION AND DECOY CARRIERS

Transportation can be a major problem when decoys are concerned. The fellow hunting the small pothole has it easiest. He can get the job done with a half dozen or so rubber inflatable decoys, which when deflated can be rolled into a compact ball and stuffed in the pocket of his hunting coat. But as pointed out earlier in this book the rubber inflatables bounce too much when the water is rough and the wind strong. Therefore under gusty conditions the hunter ought to go with sturdier decoys. The plastic inflatables have the weight to keep from bouncing and do a satisfactory job in rough weather, but you can not roll them up and stuff more than one to a pocket in a hunting coat. Some sort of sack is needed.

When deflated a dozen of these plastics will fit nicely in a newspaper carrier's bag. This bag has a wide strap that rides nicely on the shoulder without cutting into the flesh. This same bag is large enough to tote six to eight rigid plastics or cedar block decoys, depending upon the size of the blocks. Tie cords should be sewed at intervals so the wide opening of this bag can be tied shut securely to prevent loss of decoys. Since it is not always easy to find a suitable hiding place for these bags after the decoys have been set on the pond, the hunter must dye the bag either brown or black. Brown is the color of marsh growth in the winter and black is the color of mud.

Service barracks bags also make excellent decoy carriers, and since they are already dull olive drab, dark green or dull navy blue, they blend in quite well with the usual waterfowl marsh. These bags are sufficiently large to carry about a dozen and a half plastic inflatables or about a dozen rigid plastic or cedar block decoys. Full body goose decoys will go about three to a barracks bag. If the hunter goes for his geese in fields rather than on water, he should get decoy bodies that are three-quarter shells. These can be nested one atop the other, and then secured together for carrying by looping a belt or cord through the holes where the detachable heads are inserted. The heads and necks can be carried separately in a bag and will go four to five dozen in a news bag with no problems.

Tow sacks can be used, but these sacks are prone to rot and often will not last out a single season. Nylon laundry bags make good carriers but like the newspaper bag they must be dyed.

Decoys that have the colors molded into the material of manufacture can stand all sorts of abuse without showing any wear that can be noted from a distance. Decoys that have the colors painted on present an entirely different picture. They will rub together and show scratches, scrapes and mars that can be seen from a considerable distance. This problem can be eliminated by slipping each decoy into an old sock. The only problem here is the load can get mighty heavy if the socks get wet. This is very likely to happen since waterfowl hunting is seldom in dry weather.

Carrying decoys by boat certainly eliminates wear and tear on one's shoulders, but this manner of hauling has its problems, too. The blocks can either be stacked in the boat, preferably up near the bow, or put in bushel baskets which in turn are put in the boat. The main problem is to balance the load in the boat. Decoys put in bushel baskets make for easier and quicker moving if the load has to be shifted to trim the boat in rough seas, another highly likely possibility. Sacks can be used in place of baskets, but they can pick up an awful lot of weight when they get wet from rain or spray. If deep water has to be crossed in order to reach the hunting blind, baskets and sacks give the hunter the best safety margin. A heavy load of decoys can make the boat susceptible to swamping when heavy weather blows in suddenly and unexpectedly. The load can be lightened and the boat trimmed quicker if the hunter can jettison the decoys by baskets or sacks rather than by tossing blocks over individually.

The baskets and sacks as well as individual blocks will blow ashore and a good percentage of them can be retrieved after the blow. I know of a number of cases where hunters lost their lives because they could not dump deadweight decoys quick enough. One can always buy new decoys. One can not buy back life.

APPENDIX 4. TEN YARD TEST PATTERN

The standard test for shotgun patterns is a 30-inch circle at a range of 40 yards. A comparable test can be made at ten yards by using a seven-inch circle. The difference in determining the percentage of the pattern is to count the pellet hits *outside* of the circle when the seven-inch pattern is used. In the case of the standard 40-yard range the hits *inside* of the 30-inch circle are counted.

The 10-yard test provides a means of determining if the gun is sending its load to point of aim. It is easier to sight true on the center of the test circle at 10 yards than it is at four times the distance at 40 yards.

APPENDIX 5. SHOTGUN BORES AND CHOKES

Listed in the table below are shotgun bores and degrees of chokes in inches. Only shotgun gauges suitable for waterfowl hunting are covered. Under chokes are listed improved cylinder and cylinder borings. These borings are not suitable for waterfowl hunting but are listed for comparison purposes only.

Gauge	Bores	and	Chokes	in inches	
	Bore	Full choke	Modified	Imp. Cyl.	Cyl.
Ten	.775	.740	.755	.765	.775
Twelve	.729	.694	.710	.720	.729
Sixteen	.667	.639	.652	.660	.667
Twenty	.617	.592	.603	.610	.617

APPENDIX 6. SHOTGUN PELLET STATISTICS

The following table lists the weight, diameter and pellets per ounce for various shot sizes that are considered suitable for waterfowl hunting over decoys.

Shot size				
	2	4	5	6	7½
Weight in grains	4.86	3.24	2.57	1.94	1.07
Diameter in inches	.15	.13	.12	.11	.095
Pellets per ounce	90	135	170	225	350

Birdshot diameters in hundredths of an inch can be determined by subtracting the shot size number from .17. For example, No. 2 shot subtracted from .17 gives .15 as the diameter in inches.

APPENDIX 7. PATTERN PERCENTAGES

The following table lists the approximate percentage of pellets striking within a 30-inch circle. Improved cylinder and cylinder borings are unsuited for waterfowl hunting but are listed for comparison purposes only.

	Range in yards									
Degree of choke	15	20	25	30	35	40	45	50	55	60
Full	100	100	100	90	80	70	60	50	40	30
Modified	100	100	90	80	70	60	50	40	30	20
Improved cylinder	100	90	80	70	60	50	40	30	20	10
Cylinder	90	80	70	60	50	40	30	20	10	—

APPENDIX 7.
SHOT SIZE-LOAD COMBINATIONS

The table below lists approximate number of pellets hitting inside of 30-inch circle at 40 yards for full choke (70 percent) and modified (60 percent) barrels. Only shot sizes suitable for shooting over decoys and shot-size-load combinations readily obtainable are listed.

Size of load	Shot size/pellets in load				
	2	4	5	6	7½
One-ounce load	90	135	170	225	350
Full choke barrel	63	104	119	157	245
Modified barrel	54	81	102	135	210
One ⅛-ounce load	101	151	191	253	393
Full choke barrel	70	105	138	177	275
Modified barrel	60	90	114	152	236
One ¼-ounce load	112	168	212	281	437
Full choke barrel	78	118	148	197	307
Modified barrel	67	101	127	168	242
One ½-ounce load	135	141	—	—	—
Full choke barrel	95	141	—	—	—
Modified barrel	81	121	—	—	—
One ⅝-ounce load	148	219	276	365	—
Full choke barrel	104	153	193	256	—
Modified barrel	89	131	166	219	—

Size of load		Shot size/pellets in load			
Two-ounce load	180	270	340	450	—
Full choke barrel	126	189	238	315	—
Modified barrel	108	162	204	270	—

APPENDIX 8.   MAXIMUM PELLET RANGE

The most important single characteristic of a shotgun is its very limited range, which in a way is an advantage since it permits hunting in settled rural areas. With the normal loads and pellet sizes popular for waterfowl hunting, a shotgun's effective kill range is substantially less than 100 yards. This does not mean, however, that pellets will cause no damage to property or injury to persons beyond the initial 100 yards. The pellets, in fact, carry considerable distances beyond.

Near the beginning of the 20th Century, a General Journée of the French army conducted numerous experiments with sporting arms and came up with an interesting formula covering the range of shotgun pellets. His formula states that the maximum range in yards is equal to 2200 times the diameter of the lead shot pellets in inches.

The diameter of lead pellets in hundredths of an inch is reached by subtracting the shot size number from 17. For example, No. 6 shot subtracted from 17 gives 11, which in turn designates the size of the shot as .11 inches. Then by multiplying .11 by 2200 one gets 242 as the number of yards No. 6 pellets will carry. This carry range, of course, can vary considerably to either side of 242 yards according to wind velocity, wind direction, temperature and humidity.

The table that follows gives the maximum range in yards for various shot sizes used by waterfowlers.

Shot size	Diameter in inches	Maximum range in yards
No. 4 buck	.24	528
No. 3 buck	.23	506
BB	.18	396
No. 2	.15	330
No. 4	.13	286
No. 5	.12	264
No. 6	.11	242
No. 7 ½	.095	209
No. 8	.09	198

Number 3 and 4 buckshot are not recommended for waterfowl hunting. Nevertheless it is not uncommon for pass-shooters to resort to these large shot sizes on high flying geese. Consequently it is a good idea to know approximately where spent shot will fall. No. 8 shot is not a recommended size for other than close-range, over-decoy shooting on small size ducks such as teal or as "cripple-stopper" loads to dispatch wounded ducks either on land or water.

The Journée rule holds for spherical projectiles. With such a shape range is governed almost entirely by air resistance. Projectiles of other shapes have longer ranges because the shapes have less air resistance. Thus the pointed projectile goes through the air easier and will have longer range than a sphere of the same weight.

APPENDIX 9. WATERFOWL SIZES

The table below lists the approximate sizes of various species of waterfowl. Average body lengths are in inches. Extremes in wingspreads are listed in inches, and extremes in weights are listed in pounds.

Species	Body length (in inches)	Wingspread (in inches)	Weight (in pounds)
GEESE			
Canada goose	18-25	50-68	7½-15
Lesser Canada goose	16-21	45-50	5-7
Black brant	17	45-50	3-3¾
Speckle-belly goose	20	54-62	5½-7
Greater snow goose	20	53-62	5¼-6¾
Lesser snow goose	19	55-61	5¼-6¼
Blue goose	19	53-57	4¼-6¼
Ross' goose	16	44-48	2½-3¾
DUCKS			
Mallard	16	34-38	2½-5
Red-legged black duck	16	34-39	2½-4½
Black duck	16	34-36	2½-3½
Mottled duck	15	30-32	2½-3
Pintail	18	33-35	2-2¾
Gadwall	14	34-35	2-2½
Widgeon	14	30-34	1¾-2
Shoveller	14	30-34	1¼-1½
Blue-winged teal	11	24-30	¾-1
Green-winged teal	10	22-24	⅝-⅞
Wood duck	13	26-28	1¼-1½
Redhead	14	30-33	1¾-3
Canvasback	15	34-36	2¼-4¼
Ring-necked duck	12	25-28	1-1½
Greater scaup	13	29-34	1½-2¾
Lesser scaup	12	27-29	1¼-2¼
Goldeneye	13	27-31	1¾-2¾
Barrow's goldeneye	13	30-31	1¾-2¾
Bufflehead	10	22-24	¾-1¼
Ruddy duck	11	20-24	1-1½
SEA DUCKS			
Common eider	17	38-41	2¾-3¾
Oldsquaw	15	28-30	1¾-2½

Species	Body length (in inches)	Wingspread (in inches)	Weight (in pounds)
Common scoter	14	30-34	1½-2
White-winged scoter	16	35-40	1¾-3
Surf scoter	14	30-36	1½-2½
MERGANSERS			
Common merganser	18	34-39	2½-3½
Red-breasted merganser	16	32-35	2-3
Hooded merganser	12	24-26	1-1½

APPENDIX 10. WATERFOWL SPEEDS

Waterfowl fly at various speeds. Over long migration routes they move at a cruising speed that permits maximum distances with the least expenditure of energy. Their migration speed is considerably less than their top speed, which is often referred to as "escape speed" or "chased speed."

The hunter should be concerned with both of these speeds and must be prepared to make rapid allowances in how much he leads a bird if he expects to score hits. Numerous checks on waterfowl flying speeds have been made, and it is now generally accepted that most ducks and geese normally fly in a speed range between 35 and 50 miles per hour. This speed, of course, can vary considerably, plus or minus, depending upon wind velocity and wind direction. We frequently hear hunters tell of ducks buzzing across the decoys so fast they never had a chance to bring up their guns. Another person picks up the "fast-flying duck" story, and then still another relates it again, this time converting the "buzzing" to "90 miles an hour." Bird size, wind velocity and wind direction, and the bird's proximity to land or water surface can combine to create illusions of speed.

Because of its large size the Canada goose crossing at 45 miles an hour appears to be flying slow. A minute or so later a tiny green-winged teal crossing at the same 45 miles per hour seems to be moving much faster than the goose. Sizes create different impressions.

A mallard flying 50 miles per hour (air speed) can cause various speed sensations. It presents an illusion of great speed if it is skimming along just a few feet above the ground or water. The same bird at the same air speed appears to be loafing along if it is at an altitude of several hundred feet. Now add the wind. The same mallard flying directly into a 30 mile per hour wind will appear to be moving slow in relation to the ground since the head wind will reduce its ground speed to 20 miles an hour. Turn the mallard around and let it fly 50 miles per hour with the same 30 mile an hour wind as a tail wind, and we have a bird moving like "greased lightning" with a ground speed of 80 miles per hour. Just imagine the illusion of speed this bird creates when it zings past within a few feet of a hunter. The hunter who consistently bags waterfowl is one who always allows for the wind when he swings his gun to lead his target.

The following list records approximate top speeds of some ducks and geese as determined by chasing with automobile or motorcycle.

Canvasback	75 m.p.h.
Canada goose	60 m.p.h.
Mallard	60 m.p.h.
Black duck	58 m.p.h.
Snow goose	55 m.p.h.
Blue goose	55 m.p.h.
Blue-winged teal	55 m.p.h.
Shoveller	55 m.p.h.
Lesser scaup (bluebill)	52 m.p.h.
Redhead	50 m.p.h.
Mottled duck	50 m.p.h.
Green-winged teal	48 m.p.h.
Wood duck	45 m.p.h.

The speeds are all ground speeds and the records were made on days when the wind was light, 10 miles per hour or less. In all cases the flights were sudden bursts of speed and after relatively short straight flights, directions became generally erratic. Whereas ducks and geese flying at cruising speeds may wing for hours without making direction changes, those birds chased employed evasive maneuvers and turns in addition to speed to elude their pursuers. Rarely did any fly more than a half-mile before changing directions, and often that change was in a direction that prohibited continuing chase by car or motorcycle. When close pressed, most of the birds flew only about a quarter-mile before taking evasive action.

How long ducks and geese can fly at escape speed is anybody's guess. Certainly they can't do it for hours on end as in long migration flights. The author and a light plane pilot friend once chased a flight of canvasbacks for approximately 10 miles before the ducks took evasive action that the plane could not duplicate. The air speed indicator registered 90 miles an hour. True ground speed was probably closer to 75 or 80 miles an hour since the wedge of canvasbacks was flying directly into a light norther. On several other occasions we bird-dogged snow geese flights where the speed crept up to nearly 70 miles per hour. Again this was air speed, and I rather suspect true ground speed on each occasion was closer to 60 miles per hour. In none of the cases did the geese fly more than three or four miles before making sharp evasive turns.

Even in the interest of science, it is dangerous to chase either ducks or geese with an airplane. It is a violation of federal regulations to use an airplane to herd or drive waterfowl during the hunting season. In our observations in chasing waterfowl in hopes of learning something about their speeds, initial escape flight was almost always either into or quartering into the wind. Then when the birds discovered their propellered pursuer maintaining station on their tails, they broke sharply and flew downwind. It is indeed a sensation to have ducks and geese suddenly turn and come whistling past the airplane. A panicked bird could have smashed into the prop and sent us all to an early demise in the marsh below.

A point I have never been able to understand is why the birds sought initial escape flying directly into or quartering into the wind. It seems more logical, at least to the human mind, that one could vacate the premises faster by flying downwind to make the most of whatever extra push the wind could give.

APPENDIX 11. PLUMAGES AND MOULTS

Ducks are thought of in terms of vividly colored drakes (males) and rather drab and somber hued hens (females). These visions are correct, but only for a part of each year. In fact, within the life cycle of ducks, the birds go from juvenile to adult plumage in addition to changing cloaks several times during the course of the year.

The vibrant, sometimes gaudy, colors and markings worn by the drakes are the winter plumage of the birds. These are worn by the drakes through the winter and well into the breeding season. In their splendid dress the drakes become very aggressive birds where hens are concerned. If other males are in the immediate vicinity, there will be numerous fights, none fatal, however, as dominant drakes seek to win the favor of the hens.

Mallard drake at right is in full winter plumage. Juvenile drake in center is not yet in full winter dress. The mallard hen at left is in her full winter plumage.

This mallard drake is just going into winter plumage. Its head is beginning to darken and the white collar around its neck is beginning to appear.

After breeding has been completed and as soon as the hens are well into incubation chores, which is usually early summer, the drakes of most duck species lose all interest in the females and abandon them. The drakes gather in flocks and proceed to moult their bright winter plumage. The brilliantly hued coat is replaced by drab colors, which in most instances are practically identical to those found on the adult female. The term applied to this dress is "eclipse moult." This moult is a complete one of body feathers, tail feathers and flight feathers, and at its height the drakes are grounded and flightless. This flightless period covers a span of approximately three weeks in most species.

When the drakes have their flight feathers grown in again, the birds begin a second moult at which time the hen-hued plumage is gradually replaced by the rich colors of the winter plumage. This moult usually starts in early September and takes considerable time to complete. Consequently in the northern states where hunting seasons sometimes open in September the drakes will still not be in full winter plumage. Hunters not familiar with duck moult and plumage stages mistakenly consider these drakes as young birds, "this year's hatch."

This autumn moult is known as the "pre-nuptial" moult. It is a prolonged moult but only a partial one in that the wing feathers, which are renewed during the "eclipse" are not moulted again. An interesting sidelight to this is the fact that the "eclipse" is found only in the ducks of the Northern Hemisphere. This is true even in countries with climates similar to those of the Northern Hemisphere. It is also true in ducks of the same species.

The eclipse in puddle or dabbling ducks is complete whereas in the diver ducks it is less so to the extent where traces of the winter plumage are retained. There is also a difference in the flightless period. In the case of puddle ducks the flightless period is generally from early or mid-July to early August, while for the divers it usually ranges from late July until the last of August.

The moult of the adult hen in the spring is gradual and inconspicuous, and feathers dropped are replaced by others of identical color. Near the end of the moult the hen loses her inner layer of down, and this in turn is replaced with a similar coat plus special "nest down." This "nest down" is softer, longer, more strongly constructed and more resistant to moisture than the ordinary breast down. The hen later plucks this "nest down" from her breast and uses it to line the nest.

The hen undergoes still another moult, this one coming in late summer. This is a complete moult, including wing feathers, and as a result it renders the bird flightless for a period of several weeks. It is usually referred to as the "post nuptial moult," and after it is complete, the hen goes into her winter plumage.

Ducks have two moults each year, whereas geese have but one. The moult that geese undergo is a post nuptial one and one in which the entire plumage is renewed. The flight and tail feathers are shed simultaneously, and as a result the birds are flightless until the feathers are renewed. The plumage of young geese becomes full adult after the bird's second summer. Young ducks put on full adult dress when they are about 15 months old.

Hens normally nest but once a year. Nature, however, has a way of protecting its own. Should something destroy a hen's nest and eggs, the bird will generally renest. The second clutch will contain fewer fertile eggs and the hatch will be smaller than normal.

Early and late hatches account for some plumage differences in the autumn. The younger late hatch birds usually have more pin feathers, and in the case of drakes less distinct colors, than the early hatch. Late and early hatch birds, when they reach full winter plumage, which is tantamount to saying they are "young adults," can be distinguished apart only by skilled waterfowl biologists.

APPENDIX 12. HYBRID WATERFOWL

Waterfowl generally pair with others of their own kind. Nevertheless some "strange" specimens are occasionally found. These waterfowl, except in rare instances always ducks, are the results of interbreeding between different species, genera, and sub-species. This interbreeding occurs since related species often have overlapping breeding and nesting ranges. As a result, some very unusual wild hybrids occur.

The common mallard (*Anas platyrhynchos*) is worldwide in distribution and quite naturally is the species most often involved in hybridism. It crossbreeds quite readily, and then to make it even more interesting, it does so repeatedly. Consequently there occasionally appear specimens, to borrow a phrase from an old hunting guide, "colored like nothin' ever see'd befoh." Mallard crosses with black ducks, mottled ducks, pintails, gadwalls, baldpates, shovellers and green-winged teal are the more common hybrids. The wood duck has been crossed with 15 other species.

This drake is not a true mallard. It is a hybrid produced by breeding a mallard with a white Pekin. It was one of six offspring. The other five had only white Pekin markings.

Except for mallard, black duck and mottled duck crosses, the hybrids are rarely fertile. Sterility is almost 100 percent certain in hybrids derived from distantly related species. From personal experiences over a number of years of raising and banding waterfowl, the author has found hybrids to be rather fragile creatures, injury prone and susceptible to diseases.

Of what importance is hybridism to the person who hunts over decoys? To begin with the hybrids tend to disassociate themselves from the flock. They are invariably shy and frequently are secretive specimens. Not only do they tend to shy away from the flock, they also spend a lot of time in secluded areas where cover is relatively heavy. One gets the impression they are ashamed of their looks. Hence a spread of decoys improperly colored can present an unnatural scene to normal birds, with the end result that the untainted strains tend strongly to become suspicious and flare off.

It behooves the hunter who bags a hybrid to carefully preserve the bird for close examination and positive identification by a waterfowl biologist. Some hybrid strains are rare and as mounted specimens become quite valuable.

The more common hybrids are easiest to distinguish when the birds are in winter plumage. This is when the drakes stand out in all their vibrant colors. During the summer moult and at the time when the birds lose their power of flight, almost all species take on the rather drab coloration of the hens. Following the moult the birds grow new flight feathers but are slow in taking on the full colors of winter plumage. Back in years when hunting was legal in early October in the southern United States, I killed drake mallards that had only traces of green heads, white collars or rust-colored breasts. These birds were not hybrids. They were simply birds that had not yet gone into full winter plumage.

APPENDIX 13. AERIAL ANTICS

In 1967 George R. Hall, Inc., put out a calendar with an illustration of flying Canada geese. The illustration provoked all sorts of comments, questions and arguments, for one of the geese shown was flying upside down. The bird was flying on its back but with its neck twisted so that its head was in a normal position.

The illustration was not to perpetrate a hoax. Ducks and geese actually fly upside down. The "on-the-back" flights are of short duration. Numerous opinions have been recorded as to why the birds do this. The views range from "flying on their backs to rest" to "young birds just learning to fly."

From personal observations the author leans to the belief that upside down flying is part of the aerial antics connected with the courtship period. I have seen ducks, mostly mallards and teal, fly some amazing maneuvers while engaged in courtship. In all cases the birds observed performing the maneuvers were drakes. Undoubtedly their actions were to gain the attention and win the favor of females. I have never seen any hens perform similar maneuvers during the courtship period. In addition to upside down flying, which in each case was short, I have observed drakes fly tight circles around and over hens, loop the loop, barrel roll and do Immelman turns. With the exception of upside down flying and Immelman turns, I have never seen any of these maneuvers during the hunting season proper. They have only been noted in late January through early March, or up to the time the birds migrated northward to their nesting grounds.

The upside down flights and Immelman turns noted during the hunting seasons proper were, I believe, frantic escape maneuvers. In each instance the upside down flight or Immelman turn was made immediately after I fired at a bird and missed. The birds, of course, rapidly accelerated to escape speed and then followed swiftly with violently evasive action.

APPENDIX 14.
WATERFOWL DRESSING AND COOKING

Like any wild game waterfowl as tablefare are no better than the attention given them in dressing, storing and cooking. These birds have a distinct wild flavor, which some folks find objectionable. This wild flavor, which can be described as being musky or liverish, can be minimized.

The musky or liverish taste is because of the dark meat. Ducks and geese are constant flyers and birds that fly very long distances. Their powerful wings are controlled by their breast muscles which must be supplied with a steady flow of blood-carrying oxygen. Consequently the breasts of ducks and geese contain a great number of tiny veins that carry the blood. This is what makes the meat dark. Birds that do no long distance flying have white meat breasts as a result of a lesser number of veins. Examples of the white-breasted birds include pheasants, quail, and tame barnyard fowl.

Wild ducks and geese should be gutted as soon as practical. If the weather is hot, the birds should be drawn not more than an hour after killing for the meat can taint quickly when temperatures are high. Under more normal waterfowl hunting conditions, the weather is generally cold with the temperature often hovering near the freezing mark. When these conditions exist, there is no harm to the meat if the gutting takes place several hours after killing.

After the fowl is drawn it should be hung to drain for about 15 minutes. If running water is available, it is advisable to flush out the cavity before hanging the bird to drain. After the bird has drained, it should be dried with a dish cloth and put under refrigeration until it can be plucked and completely cleaned for table use. If the fowl is to be eaten at a later date, it should be securely wrapped, labeled with date of wrapping and then quick frozen for storage.

For those who dislike the wild flavor of waterfowl, the taste can be minimized by skinning the birds just prior to cooking. The skin should be left on the bird while it is in cold storage as it is good protection against freezer burn.

There are scores of waterfowl recipes—simple as well as fancy—from which to choose. The following are just a few simple tasty recipes.

BROILED DUCK BREASTS

Two to six ducks, depending on size; two to six strips of bacon; butter, salt and pepper. Place ducks, breast side up, in broiling pan. Slice breast meat parallel with breast bone once on each side for small ducks, twice for large birds. Insert thin slice of butter into each slit, salt and pepper and wrap each bird with strip of bacon. Broil until done. Bacon and butter give duck meat juicier texture and help to cover up wild taste. Gravy can be made with the drippings. Two large mallard-size or six small teal-size ducks will serve four.

DUCKS IN SOUR CREAM

Two to six ducks, depending on size; flour; oil or butter; salt and pepper; beef or poultry stock or water; one cup sour cream; three to four slices of bacon. Wash and dry birds thoroughly. Salt and pepper, roll in flour and brown lightly in oil or butter. Place bacon strips in casserole and partly cooked birds on top. Pour over this just enough beef or poultry stock, or water if the stock is not available, to prevent sticking. Cover and cook for one hour in oven at 350 degrees. Pour sour cream over the fowl ten minutes before serving. Two large mallard-size or six small teal-size ducks will serve four.

BARBECUED DUCK

Two large mallard-size or six small teal-size duck breasts; four teaspoons lemon juice; one teaspoon catsup; one teaspoon Worcestershire sauce; one tablespoon butter; salt and paprika. Broil breasts until brown and baste frequently with barbecue sauce made from other ingredients. After meat has begun to brown, sprinkle with salt and paprika and continue to broil until meat is cooked to desired degree. Serves four.

GEESE

The broiled breasts, sour cream and barbeque recipes listed for ducks will serve for the smaller geese that dress out at three to four pounds. One goose will serve four people. Larger geese that dress out in excess of five pounds are tastier when baked or roasted.

ROAST GOOSE WITH DRESSING

One large goose; salt and pepper; lemon juice and butter. For dressing: loaf of day-old bread, one can chicken broth, six slices bacon diced, two medium onions chopped, two green peppers chopped, one-half cup butter, one teaspoon baking powder, three stalks celery chopped, one-third cup parsley, thyme or sage. To prepare dressing soften crumbed bread in chicken broth. Fry bacon until almost brown. Add onions, celery, peppers, giblets and butter. Fry until all are tender. Add to bread. Add baking powder, parsley and seasonings, and if dressing is not moist enough, add a little water. Place in greased pan and set inside a larger pan containing water. Cover with aluminum foil and bake 1½ hours at 350 degrees. Keep adding water to outer pan. To roast the goose, clean the fowl and rub body cavity with salt and lemon juice. Pile the dressing lightly inside and truss the fowl by closing the cavity with skewers and lace with clean white string back and forth as in lacing a shoe. Fold wing tips under the bird. Tie ends of legs with string and bring this down around the tailpiece. All strings and skewers must be removed before serving. Preheat oven to 350 degrees. Place fowl, breast up, in roasting pan. Brush with melted butter and lemon juice. Sprinkle with salt and pepper. Brown in oven and then cover with roaster cover or aluminum foil. Reduce the heat to 300 degrees and roast 20 minutes for each pound. If the fowl is stuffed with dressing, add an extra ten minutes roasting. Baste frequently with ¼ cup butter melted in a cup of boiling water. When this is used up, continue to baste with the juice in the roaster.

APPENDIX 15. BANDED WATERFOWL

A high point in the life of every waterfowl hunter is the bagging of a banded bird. There are many who hunt a lifetime and never kill a banded duck or goose. Yet there are others who collect banded birds on their first hunts.

Bird banding is conducted by federal, state and provincial conservation agencies as well as thousands of professional and amateur ornithologists. The obvious purpose of bands is to learn more about bird habits, lives and migrations. The banding program has a special meaning for the waterfowl hunter, since the reports aid in setting the basis for seasons, bag and possession limits. Consequently it is to the hunter's advantage to file a report on every band he collects. The address of where to file the report is included on the band. The hunter keeps the band and just sends in the band number, date and place of kill.

In the case of waterfowl, most bands are aluminum rings that are attached to the leg of the bird. In recent years, however, brightly colored plastic neck bands have been used, mostly in the banding of geese. These bands are easy to see and they enable trained waterfowl biologists to follow closely bird movements either on nesting or wintering grounds. Up through 1971 the number of banded birds, all species, was in excess of 19 million. Permanent files on these bands are kept at the Migratory Bird Populations Station at Laurel, Maryland.

Hunters filing reports on banded birds receive certificates of appreciation from the Maryland station. The certificate includes such data as name of bander, place and date of banding, species and age of bird. The longer a bird carries the band, the more interesting the story that unfolds from the banding report.

For example, consider the first snow goose my youngest daughter bagged on Jan. 9, 1972. It was a lesser snow goose carrying band number 667-57586. The banding report returned to Laura noted the bird had been banded on Aug. 1, 1962. Since date of kill was Jan. 9, 1972, a little arithmetic showed the bird as carrying the band for nine and a half years. The average life span of banded waterfowl is about five to six years. Laura's goose was well beyond the average. The banding report also noted that the age of the bird was unknown at the time of banding by the Canadian Wildlife Service. This indicated that the bird at banding time was at least a year to a year and a half old. A snow goose is easily identified as a juvenile in this period since its feathers are distinctively grey in tinge to give the bird an overall "dirty white" appearance. Geese return to the same breeding and wintering grounds each year. Laura's goose was banded near Eskimo Point in the Keewatin District of Canada's Northwest Territories and it was killed on the Barrow Hunting Preserve in Texas. Multiplying out the number of round trips that bird made in its known nine and a half years gave the goose a migratory travel log of some 70,000 miles. And this does not include mileage logged on those daily "local" flights on nesting and wintering grounds.

These known facts in turn breed some interesting questions. How many times did the bird work to decoys? How often was the bird fired upon by hunters? Was the bird ever wounded in its lifetime? How many young did it raise? One could go on and on with interesting questions. What makes it even more interesting is the fact that the bird was juicy and tender. By rights a nine and a half year old goose ought to be tough. Apparently my wife did a good job in preparing it for the table.

Glossary

AUTOLOADER: Type of shotgun that automatically ejects empty shell, reloads live shell and fires each time trigger is pulled; full automatic is weapon that fires continuously as long as trigger is held down; full automatic guns are illegal in waterfowl hunting.

BAG LIMIT: Number of ducks and geese hunter can take in a single day.

BAITING: Spreading of food to attract waterfowl; this practice is illegal in modern waterfowl hunting.

BLIND: Any cover or structure a hunter uses for concealment.

BLOCK: Old term used for a decoy; term stems from early days when decoys were often little more than oblong blocks of wood.

BORE: Measurement of shotgun barrels; it is measurement of inside diameter of the barrel.

BRASS: Bottom portion of shotgun shell housing detonator cap and powder.

CALL: Device, blown or hand operated, used to call and attract waterfowl; electronic calling devices are illegal in waterfowl hunting.

CALLER DUCKS: Tame ducks trained to call wildfowl; use of caller ducks now illegal.

CAP: Primer or detonator in shotgun shell.

CAP-BUSTER: Hunter who repeatedly shoots at game far out of range.

CHOKE: Constriction of shotgun muzzle to control spread of shot.

CHOP: Wave action in rough water.

CONCENTRATION: Term applied to huge masses of waterfowl.

CONFIDENCE DECOY: Replica of bird species that give waterfowl confidence to approach close to decoy spread.

COVER: Materials utilized in screening hunter from sight; also a blind.

CRIPPLE-STOPPER: Load of small size pellets for dense pattern to score head and neck hits on cripple birds on water.

DABBLERS: Duck species that feed in or frequent shallow water; puddle duck species.

DAY HUNTING CAMP: Camp that sells hunting rights on a daily basis as opposed to a private club or camp that leases out hunting rights by the season.

DIPPER DECOY: Specialized type of decoy that dips head and bill in water when activating line to blind is pulled.

DIVERS: Ducks skilled in diving, species usually distinguished by low-on-the-water profile.

DOWN: Soft feathers on belly and underside of waterfowl.

DRAKE: A male duck.

DROVE: Small flight of ducks.

EFFECTIVE RANGE: Range within which waterfowl can be killed consistently; outside limit of effective range is usually five to eight yards less than maximum range.

FEEDER DECOY: Decoy arranged to imitate feeding duck or goose.

FIELD LOAD: Standard shotgun load or shell.

FLYWAY: Paths that birds follow in their migrations; four major North American flyways are Atlantic, Mississippi, Central and Pacific; on breeding and wintering grounds waterfowl have local flyways between roosts and feeding areas.

FLOCK SHOOTER: Hunter who shoots into flock of birds without picking a specific target; flock-shooting is good way to miss consistently.

GAGGLE: Small number of geese when not in flight; term can be applied to several families of geese; when families number in the hundreds, the gathering becomes a concentration.

GANDER: A male goose.

GAUGE: Bore measurement of shotgun barrels.

HIDE: A hunting blind.

HIGH BRASS: High power or heavy shotgun shell load.

HIGH VELOCITY LOAD: Same as high brass.

HORN: A waterfowl call.

HULL: Shotgun shell casing.

JUMP-SHOOTING: Practice of walking up ducks and shooting them as they jump off ponds.

KEEL: Weighted strip on bottom of decoy to prevent it from overturning in wind or rough water.

KILL RANGE: Same as effective range.

LEAD: Distance hunter shoots ahead of flying waterfowl so that bird and shot column meet.

LIMIT: Maximum number of birds hunter can have in his possession.

LIVE DECOYS: Use of live birds for decoy purposes; practice is now illegal.

LOW BRASS: Same as field load.

MAGNUM: Extra heavy shotgun shell.

MANDIBLE: Bill of waterfowl.

MARKET HUNTER: One who shoots wild waterfowl for sale. Practice is outlawed and market hunting is now a federal offense.

MEAT HUNTER: Term formerly applied to market hunter; term today is applied to persons unsportsmanlike in their hunting.

MEAT SHOT: Easy shot at birds on water or at rest; a shot in which a number of birds are killed; an unsportsmanlike shot.

MIXED RIG: A decoy formation including both puddler and diver duck decoys.

NAIL: Tip end of top of waterfowl's bill.

OVER LEAD: Too much lead in shooting; shot column passes in front of bird.

OVER SHOOT: Same as over lead.

PASS-SHOOTING: Shooting at flying waterfowl by getting into a local flyway.

PATTERN: Spread of shotgun pellets within a specific diameter circle at a given range; patterns are percentage of pellets striking within a 30-inch diameter circle at a range of 40 yards.

POP-UP DECOY: Type of decoy that when unfolded pops-up into semi-full or full body.

POTHOLE: Very small pond, usually big enough for not more than two or three ducks; highly favored by certain puddler duck species such as mallards and teal.

POT SHOT: A very easy shot; shot at bird at rest on water or land.

PREEN: Bird's way of trimming and dressing its feathers with its bill; practice is observed most frequently after birds have passed through a heavy rain or at end of a long migration flight.

PUDDLERS: Duck species that frequent small ponds and shallow water; same as dabblers.

RAFT: Concentration of waterfowl in dense masses on water.

RANGE DECOY: Decoy set out to indicate maximum shotgun range; a guide to when flying ducks or geese pass within range.

REST AREA: Area closed to shooting for specific purpose of allowing birds to rest; these areas are important in keeping birds in heavily hunted regions.

RIG: Term applied to spread of decoys.

ROOST: Area where birds congregate to spend the night.

SHELL: A round of ammunition for shotgun.

SHOT COLUMN: As soon as compact mass of pellets leaves shotgun muzzle, the shot begins to string out in a column; at 40 yards column usually measures 15 to 20 feet in length from leading pellets to trailing pellets.

SHOT STRING: Same as shot column.

SLEEPER DECOY: Decoy made to resemble a sleeping bird.

STOOL: When live decoys were legal, stool was placed in water for

decoys to climb onto to rest; old term used to describe waterfowl
coming into the decoys.

WATERLOGGED: Porous object so soaked with water that it sinks.

WHIFFLE: Action of a decoying bird as it veers with the wind.

Bibliography

Allen, Durwood. *Our Wildlife Legacy*. New York: Funk and Wagnalls, 1954.

Amber, John T. (editor). *Gun Digest*. Chicago: The Gun Digest, 1968.

Barber, Joel. *Wild Fowl Decoys*. New York: Garden City Publishing Co., Inc., 1937.

Becker, A. C., Jr. *Waterfowl in the Marshes*. South Brunswick, N.J.: A. S. Barnes and Co., Inc., 1969.

Bent, Arthur Cleveland. *Life Histories of North American Waterfowl*. New York: Dover Publications, Inc., 1951.

Buckingham, Nash. *Game Bag*. New York: G. P. Putnam's Sons, 1945.

Bourjaily, Vance. *The Unnatural Enemy*. New York: Dial Press, 1963.

Claflin, Bert. *American Waterfowl*. New York: Alfred A. Knopf, 1952.

Connett, Eugene V., III. *Duck Decoys*. New York: D. Van Nostrand Co., 1953.

Connett, Eugene V., III (editor). *Wildfowling in the Mississippi Flyway*. New York: D. Van Nostrand Co., 1949.

Cramond, Michael. *Hunting and Fishing in North America*. Norman, Okla.: University of Oklahoma Press, 1953.

Dalrymple, Byron. *The Fundamentals of Fishing and Hunting*. New York: Pocket Books, Inc., 1959.

Day, Albert E. *North American Waterfowl*. Harrisburg, Pa.: Stackpole and Heck, Inc., 1949.

Evanoff, Vlad. *Hunting Secrets of the Experts*. Garden City, New York: Doubleday and Co., Inc., 1964.

Field and Stream Reader. Garden City, New York: Doubleday and Co., Inc., 1946.

Godfrey, Joe Jr., and Dufresne, Frank (editors). *The Great Outdoors*. New York: McGraw-Hill Co., Inc., 1949.

Grange, Wallace Byron. *The Way to Game Abundance*. New York: Charles Scribner's Sons, 1949.

Haynes, William Barber. *Goose and Duck Shooting*. San Antonio, Texas: Naylor Co., 1961.

Hazelton, W. C. *Tales of Duck and Goose Shooting*. Chicago: Eastman Brothers Press, 1916.

Holland, Ray P. *Scattergunning*. New York: Alfred A. Knopf, 1951.

Heilner, Van Campen. *A Book on Duck Shooting*. New York: Alfred A. Knopf, 1947.

Hockbaum, H. Albert. *Travels and Traditions of Waterfowl*. Minneapolis: University of Minnesota Press, 1955.

Janes, Edward C. *Hunting Ducks and Geese*. Harrisburg, Pa.: Stackpole Co., 1954.

Kortwright, Francis H. *The Ducks, Geese and Swans of North America*. Washington: American Wildlife Institute, 1942.

Labisky, Wallace R. *Waterfowl Shooting*. New York: Greenberg Publishing, 1954

Linduske, Joseph P. (editor) : Washington, D.C.: *Waterfowl Tomorrow,* U. S. Department of the Interior, 1964.

MacKenty, John G. *Duck Hunting*. New York: A. S. Barnes and Co., Inc., 1953.

Mackey, William J. *American Bird Decoys*. New York: E. P. Dutton and Co., Inc., 1965.

Madson, John. *The Mallard*. East Alton, Ill.: Olin Mathieson Chemical Corp., 1960.

Orvington, Ray (editor). *The Compact Book of Waterfowl and Lowland Game Birds*. New York: J. Lowell Pratt and Co., 1965.

Phillips, John C., and Lincoln, Frederick C. *American Waterfowl—Their Present Situation and the Outlook for the Future*. New York: Houghton Mifflin Co., 1930.

Parmalee, Paul W., and Loomis, Forrest D. *Decoys and Decoy Carvers of Illinois*. DeKalb, Ill.: Northern Illinois University Press, 1969.

Rikhoff, Jim (editor). *The Compact Book of Hunting*. New York: J. Lowell Pratt and Co., 1964.

Ripley, Dillon. *A Paddling of Ducks*. New York: Harcourt, Brace and Co., 1957.

Stefferud, Alfred (editor). *Birds in Our Lives*. Washington, D.C.: U. S. Department of The Interior, 1966.

Stilwell, Hart. *Hunting and Fishing in Texas*. New York: Alfred A. Knopf, 1946.

Stringfellow, Robert B. (editor). *The Standard Book of Hunting and Fishing*. Harrisburg, Pa.: Stackpole and Heck, 1950.

Trueblood, Ted *The Hunter's Handbook*. New York: Thomas Y. Crowell Co., 1954.

Wing, Leonard W. *Natural History of Birds*. New York: The Ronald Press, 1956.

Wulff, Lee (editor). *The Sportsman's Companion*. New York: Harper and Row, 1968.

Index